"The good Lord wants
The book you are holdi
trust God and how to k(
your heart and let Him
wants to lead you throu

from the foreword by George Foreman,
former two-time World Heavyweight Boxing Champion

"Solomon said, 'The writing of many books is endless.' Books are continually coming out on nearly every subject in the world, so which ones should you read? If you want to get rid of your worry, you need to read this book. It is unlikely you will ever read the very important information in this book anywhere else. I believe the character of the author makes the content of the book even more valuable. Kent is a man of godly character, so I highly recommend the reading of this vitally important subject."

Peter Lord,
bestselling author, *Hearing God*

"Kent is a man of great passion for God—teachable, diligent, pristine in character, a faithful friend of God who administers spiritual life support to those entrusted to him. Kent trusts God as one hundred percent sovereign. He lives what he writes."

Jean Krisle Blasi,
founder and president, Kingdom Crafstman Ministries;
author, *Prophetic Fishing*

THE SURE
CURE
FOR WORRY

THE SURE CURE FOR WORRY

Learning to Trust God
No Matter What Happens

KENT CROCKETT

Chosen
a division of Baker Publishing Group
Minneapolis, Minnesota

© 2013 by Kent Crockett

Published by Chosen Books
11400 Hampshire Avenue South
Bloomington, Minnesota 55438
www.chosenbooks.com

Chosen Books is a division of
Baker Publishing Group, Grand Rapids, Michigan

Printed in the United States of America

Library of Congress Cataloging-in-Publication Data
Crockett, Kent
      The sure cure for worry : learning to trust God no matter what happens / Kent Crockett ; foreword by George Foreman.
          pages cm
      Includes bibliographical references.
      Summary: "Pastor reveals two key things that can eradicate worry in your life and help you face the future without fear, no matter what happens"—Provided by publisher.
      ISBN 978-0-8007-9553-5 (pbk. : alk. paper)
      1. Trust in God—Christianity. 2. Obedience—Religious aspects—Christianity. 3. Worry—Religious aspects—Christianity. I. Title.
      BV4637.C75 2013
      248.8′6—dc23   2013010811

Cover design by Kirk DouPonce, DogEared Design

The Author is represented by Les Stobbe, Literary Agent.

13 14 15 16 17 18 19   7 6 5 4 3 2 1

To my son, Scott, my daughter, Hannah,
and my son-in-law, Clay.

"Don't worry about tomorrow, because tomorrow
will worry about itself."

—Jesus (Matthew 6:34 HCSB)

Contents

Contents

Foreword

I did not think much about God as I was growing up in Houston. I spent most of my days and nights on the streets, getting into trouble. Mom did not have time to attend church when I was a boy because she was always working to support her seven children. Even so, she did want us to learn about God.

I remember one day she gave me a Bible and said, "George, go to your room and read this." I went to my room, flipped through the pages and looked at the pictures.

Later, when I came out of my room, she said, "Don't you feel better now?"

"Oh yeah, Mom," I lied. "I feel so much better now."

That was the extent of my Bible training growing up.

Religion was boring to me. I thought it was just an escape for poor people and little old ladies. I wanted nothing to do with that church stuff. I believed there was a God, but I did not need religion.

God got a hold of my life in 1977 and I have been serving Him ever since then. As I look back over my life, I can see how He has led and guided me through difficult times. Everyone needs help from above, including you.

The good Lord wants you to experience the best life possible. The book you are holding in your hands will show why you can trust God and how to keep from worrying. I hope you will open your heart and let Him show you that He is alive today—and wants to lead you through this life.

George Foreman,
two-time World Heavyweight Boxing Champion;
Olympic gold medalist; King of the Grills

Acknowledgments

I would like to give special thanks to the following:

My precious wife, Cindy. You have been my wife, best friend, mother of our children, counselor to the needy, my personal editor and the one who has loved me at all times. Where would I be without you? I shudder to think about that. I married way above my head.

Mike and Laurie Mozingo and the elders, staff and members of Journey Church in Prattville, Alabama. It is a joy being on the same team with you and serving God together.

George Foreman. I enjoyed watching you in the boxing ring, but what you are doing to reach people with God's love is more exciting. Thank you for writing the foreword for this book.

My agent, Les Stobbe. Thank you for your wisdom and representing me in an ever-changing publishing world.

My mentor, Peter Lord. You have taught me much about God and life, my friend. Much more than you realize.

My friends Paul and Debby Baskin. Cindy and I cherish your friendship. We have shared many laughs and tears as we have run the race of life. Thank you for your encouraging words during the tough times.

Jane Campbell, Natasha Sperling, Carra Carr, Tim Peterson, Elisa Tally, Stacey Theesfield, Ellen Chalifoux and the entire team at Chosen Books for the wonderful work you do to further God's kingdom.

PART 1

LEARNING TO TRUST GOD

Imagine you are at a football game and your team is losing by two points. The team you are cheering is on the other team's twenty-yard line with the clock stopped. One second is left in the game. The kicker runs from the bench to the field and all he has to do is kick the field goal to win the game.

Only one problem. The kicker is terrible! He has missed most of his kicks all year long. All the fans rooting for your team are nervous and worried. The spectators are chewing their fingernails or have buried their heads in their hands. Someone moans, "He is going to miss this one, too!"

Why are they worried? They do not trust the kicker.

Now let's consider another scenario. Same situation, but a different kicker comes in for the final play. This player is an All-American and has never missed a field goal all season. The fans start giving each other high fives because they know he will make the kick.

Why are they not worried? They trust the kicker.

Here is the real kicker. Worry is a trust issue. We worry because we do not trust that God is in control of our situation. We believe that He will fail us in our time of need.

Worry never trusts—and trust never worries. You cannot worry and trust God at the same time. Since trust forces out worry, you can be cured of worry by placing your complete trust in God. Before you can do that, you must be convinced that He exists, can change circumstances and cares about you. After all, why would you want to put your trust in the Lord if you do not believe He can intervene in your situation?

In the next few chapters I will present evidence proving that God is in control and is actively involved in our lives today. You cannot stop worrying by trying to talk yourself out of it. You must learn how to trust the invisible God.

1

Trusting in an Invisible God

I don't know if we each have a destiny or if we're all
just floating around accidental-like on a breeze, but
I, I think maybe it's both. Maybe both is happening
at the same time.

—Forrest Gump

Do you get a sick feeling in your stomach whenever you think
about the future? Are you terrified that an economic collapse
or some other tragedy will happen? Are you panicking because
you think that you will never find the right person to marry?
The list of things to worry about has no end. How is it possible
to live in this uncertain world without worrying?

The only way you can face the future without fear is to believe
that God is in control of your life and to learn how to be guided
by Him. No matter how confusing or desperate your situation
may be, God wants to lead you through life and provide all you

need to live. The Lord can even maneuver you to a specific place *without you knowing it* to accomplish His plan. Consider the following bizarre incident that happened to a friend of mine.

When Pete Shultis was 26 years old, his fiancée, Linda, invited him to attend a worship service at a Baptist church in Huntington, West Virginia. Pete did not want to go, but Linda kept insisting they attend because she had promised a friend they would be there. He had never been to that church before, which was in another city, but gave in due to her persistence. Little did he realize that his reluctant visit to an unfamiliar church would be like starring in an episode of *The Twilight Zone*.

They pulled up to a white stucco building, which was located in the residential Guyandotte neighborhood. A girls choir was singing that evening as part of the service before the evangelist would preach the sermon. As Pete was watching the piano player to his right, a voice spoke to his mind: *You are going to marry the girl on the far left end of the choir.*

Pete turned to see who was singing at that spot in the choir. At the left end was a slender, curly-haired brunette who appeared to be about 16 years old. She was standing next to a slightly larger girl who looked like her, and could have been her sister.

Those were the most bizarre words he had ever heard in his life! Marry a teenage choir girl he had never met before? He was already engaged to the woman seated next to him! They were in love. He had no intentions of marrying anyone else. Why would a crazy thought like that even enter his mind? Yet the words were so clear and cutting that he could not deny he heard them. But was it the devil speaking to him, or was it a message from God?

Was that You, Lord? Pete prayed. *She's just a 16-year-old high school kid. I'm 26 years old. I thought I was supposed to marry Linda. Is this some kind of test?*

Pete did not hear a reply to his question, so he asked again for an explanation.

God, I don't get this. Did I just conjure up that thought in my mind? Could it be that I'm just afraid to marry Linda? If that really was You speaking to me, how on earth could I ever date that girl? I'm too old for her.

Again, Pete did not receive an answer to his questions. He could not pay attention to the sermon that night because that strange message kept echoing in his mind. After the service ended, he made no attempt to meet the girl in the choir. He and Linda slipped out the door, and what seemed to be words from either the Lord or the devil were soon forgotten.

Several weeks passed. As Pete and Linda continued to plan their wedding, they started feeling uneasy about their decision to marry. They had been feeling uncomfortable with each other but could not pinpoint a reason why. Although they had not been fighting, their relationship was strained and did not seem to be working anymore. Something was not right. Linda suggested they call off the wedding. Pete reluctantly admitted that it was probably the right thing to do.

Shortly after their breakup, Pete moved to Charleston, West Virginia, to become the associate pastor at the Perrow Memorial Presbyterian Church. He felt like half his world had been taken away with nothing to replace it. Maybe given a little time, their feelings would change and he and Linda could get back together. It did not happen.

As he continued to minister as a single man for the next few years, the ache of loneliness only grew worse. In spite of all his best efforts to find a wife, not a single dating relationship ever worked out. One lonely night he sat down and calculated that he had seriously dated thirteen women since leaving high school, and they had all married the next man they dated after him. He was an expert at finding wives for "the next guy" but not for himself.

With each passing birthday, Pete got a little more depressed. Nearly eight years had passed since he had moved to Charleston and now he was still single at the age of 34. Whenever he was with his close friends, he would grab his right cheek and sarcastically announce, "The bait is getting older!"

One day a woman drove into the Perrow Church parking lot. At the same time, Pete pulled into the parking space right beside her. He introduced himself and found out her name was Robin. She had been thinking about attending the church and had made an appointment to meet with the senior pastor to ask a few questions.

Pete invited her into the church and showed her to the pastor's office. After getting her questions answered, she began attending the worship services there.

Over the next month, Pete and Robin struck up a cordial friendship. Pete shared his life story with her and was pleased to find out that she was single. As they continued talking to each other each Sunday, Pete wondered if maybe he had finally met the right woman to marry.

Three months later, Robin invited Pete to an Easter service at her home church in Huntington, which was about an hour's drive from Charleston. Pete's mind suddenly flashed back to when he visited a church in Huntington eight years earlier and saw the young choir girl. He had not thought about her since then.

Is it possible that Robin is the same girl in the choir that the voice pointed out eight years ago? he wondered.

Pete did not want to jump too quickly to conclusions. He cleared his throat. "Your old church is in Huntington?" he asked cautiously. "I'm just curious what the church building looks like."

"Well, it's a white stucco building in the Guyandotte neighborhood."

Pete gulped. *Settle down,* he told himself. *There must be at least five white stucco churches in that neighborhood.*

He probed further. "Did your church ever have a youth choir, like the one we have here at Perrow?" he asked.

"Oh yes," she replied. "We were called the Gospel Teens and I sang in the choir as a junior and senior in high school."

Pete's heart almost stopped.

I remember she stood at the end of the row next to a taller girl who looked like her.

"Do you happen to remember where your place was in the choir and who the person was next to you?"

Robin looked at him curiously, trying to figure out why that would matter. "I sang at the end of the row. I always stood next to my sister, Brenda, who helped me stay on key."

This is unbelievable, Pete told himself. *She's got to be the same girl the voice pointed out. She's 24, which would be about the right age, but I can't be absolutely certain until I see if it's the same church I visited eight years ago.*

As Pete drove, Robin started giving him directions to the church when they arrived in Huntington. She told him to drive down Buffington Street. "Here it is on the left," she said.

They pulled up to the same white stucco building that he had visited with Linda eight years before. Pete's jaw dropped as he stared ahead in disbelief. *It's the same church. Robin was the choir girl. It really was God speaking to me that night!*

The odds of this happening were too astronomical to be a mere coincidence. Only God could have spoken those words to his mind about his future wife and brought them together years later without either of them planning it.

Pete was jumping up and down inside, like a schoolboy getting to date the head cheerleader. Although it was tempting to tell Robin the entire story, he knew the timing was not right. He had not known her very long, and telling her might be too much for her to handle and could scare her away.

He kept the incredible incident to himself the entire time they dated. It was not until he proposed to her and she accepted that he finally shared the amazing words God had spoken to him eight years before: *You are going to marry the girl on the far left end of the choir.*

Pete Shultis and Robin Nance were joined together in marriage on March 7, 1981, and have been serving the Lord in ministry ever since.[1]

How did God make that happen? It is really quite simple. He has a plan, knows the future and He can direct our steps without our being aware of it. We will look at these aspects in more detail throughout this book, but here is a quick analysis of their situation.

1. *God had a plan for Pete and Robin to get married.* They had both given their lives to the Lord before they had ever met. God will reveal His plan to you when you are submitted to doing His will. He arranged for Pete to travel to Robin's church from another city to get a preview of his future wife.

2. *God found a way to get Pete to visit the church, even though he did not want to go.* Pete was unwilling to go but gave in to Linda's insistence. This shows that the Lord can lead people to appointed places at the right time, even when they do not want to go there.

3. *God knew Pete was engaged to the wrong woman, so He planted a thought in his mind, showing him the right person.* The Lord will speak ideas to your mind, which is one of the ways He will guide you. He spoke so clearly to Pete that the words were unmistakable and he could recall them eight years later.

4. *God halted the marriage of Pete to Linda.* The broken engagement greatly disappointed both of them, but it was actually a blessing in disguise. When God closes a door, it can appear to be the worst thing that could ever happen to you. It is usually not until later that you will discover the worst thing was really the best thing that could have happened.

5. *During the eight years of waiting, God would not allow a single dating relationship to work for Pete.* Although it

did not seem like it at the time, the Lord was doing Pete a favor by blocking his dating relationships. You must keep trusting God when He withholds what you want, knowing He has something better in mind.

6. *Eight years later, the Lord guided Robin to the exact place where Pete worked, without her being aware that she was being led.* Pete had to wait eight years before he saw the fulfillment of what the Lord had spoken to him. This shows that God's timing is often later than what we would like. Even though Pete could not understand why he needed to wait so long, the Lord knew Robin needed to grow up and mature before she was ready to meet him. In God's perfect timing, He brought them together.

Pete and Robin's story gives us a glimpse of God being in control and guiding their steps. If the Lord did it for them, He can also do it for you.

You might be wondering, *Will God control my circumstances, too? Can He guide my steps? Does He know what I am going through right now? Is He concerned about the things that worry me?*

All those questions will be addressed in this book. But first, I have a question for you. If you truly believed God knew what was best for you, would you be willing to let Him guide you through life, even if at times it did not make sense to you?

Jesus came to give you an abundant, joyful life, which cannot be experienced if you are constantly worrying. To experience the wonderful life He has planned for you, you must first learn to trust Him.

Placing Your Trust in a God You Cannot See

If you are going to place your life in God's hands and trust Him with your future, *you have to believe* that He is in control.

Think about it. Why would you want to trust God if He has no ability to control what happens to you? If He is not in control, Forrest Gump was right and we are all just "floating around accidental-like on a breeze."

The truth is, God certainly is in control and it can be proven. He has provided convincing evidence through the many prophecies in the Bible which have already been fulfilled in history, exactly as the prophets predicted.

> If you are going to place your life in God's hands and trust Him with your future, **you have to believe** that He is in control.

When you calculate the odds of these future events being foretold and later coming to pass, you will discover it would have been impossible for them to have occurred by mere chance. Those predictions—made by the Old Testament prophets and recorded in manuscripts—came from a sovereign God who knows all future events and controlled the circumstances that brought them to pass. We will examine some of these prophecies in detail in another chapter.

The Lord has given more evidence of His sovereignty through the miracles that have occurred in many people's lives, the testimonies of countless divine appointments and the overwhelming number of answered prayers. However, this does not mean you will never have questions, or that all your prayers will be answered exactly like you wish.

Many times when I have prayed, it seemed like my requests were falling on deaf ears. God normally does not make His presence obvious. We must walk through this life by faith. We are learning to trust in an invisible God whom we will not see until after we die. Yet every now and then, He will give us a bit of proof that He is right there with us and listening to our prayers.

When my daughter, Hannah, was in grade school, she wanted to join the Girl Scouts. At that time I was pastor of a small congregation and was working a part-time job to make ends meet. Buying a Girl Scout uniform did not fit into our budget, but we did not want to break her heart. Instead of telling her no, I asked her to pray about it.

"Hannah, if you're supposed to be in Girl Scouts," I said, "God will provide a uniform for you. Why don't you pray and ask Him for one?"

She went into her bedroom and prayed to the Lord for Him to give her a Girl Scout uniform.

> We are learning to trust in an invisible God whom we will not see until after we die.

Two minutes later the phone rang. The woman on the other end of the phone said, "You don't know me, but I have a Girl Scout uniform that I would like to give away. Do you have a daughter who needs one?"

For a few seconds, I was so stunned I did not even know what to say. *Is this really happening?* I wondered. *Just two minutes ago Hannah prayed for a uniform. This is impossible!*

I snapped out of it and answered, "Uh, yes, as a matter of fact, we do have a daughter who needs a uniform. I know you'll probably find this hard to believe, but she just prayed two minutes ago for a Girl Scout uniform and then you called. Your phone call is a direct answer to a child's prayer."

What are the chances that a woman who did not know us would call with the answer to Hannah's request just seconds after she prayed? Again, the odds are just too great to be a coincidence. A higher power had to be involved.

How did the Lord arrange this answer to prayer? The woman had a uniform she decided to give away instead of selling or throwing away. Next, she somehow got our name, rather than someone else's, through a miscellaneous contact. The Lord kept her from calling our house until Hannah prayed for the uniform, and then He prompted her to make the phone call immediately after Hannah's prayer. Hannah joined the Girl Scouts and wore the free uniform from heaven, which fit perfectly.

You might be asking yourself why God would answer a prayer for a uniform while millions of suffering people are not getting their prayers answered.

To be honest, I cannot tell you why. I cannot explain why some prayers are answered while others are not. It is not up to me to figure all that out. I just know it happened.

Perhaps the Lord responded to her childlike faith and wanted my little girl to know that He heard her and could answer her prayers. Maybe God wanted to prove to the woman who called that He really exists. Maybe He answered that prayer because He knew I would write about it in this book, so that thousands of readers would be inspired to pray about everything, including the small stuff. Maybe He just wanted to do something that I was not expecting and watch my reaction!

In case it escaped your notice, God did not answer the prayer by dropping a uniform from the sky. He used some humans to get it done. The woman supplied the uniform and made the phone call. My daughter said the prayer and asked God to provide for her. I answered the phone. The Lord supernaturally controlled the event, but people carried out the actions.

His guidance works the same way. He brings people and circumstances together to make things happen, sometimes without anyone knowing that He was involved.

Following God's Lead

Probably the most quoted phrase of assurance is "God is in control." Did you know that no verse in the Bible actually says that? However, when you read the Scriptures, it becomes obvious that "the LORD has established His throne in the heavens, and His sovereignty rules over all" (Psalm 103:19). Four times the book of Daniel tells us, "The Most High is ruler over the realm of mankind" (4:17, 25, 32; 5:21). And we can clearly see His hand at work in the lives of Joseph, Esther and Jesus, proving that He was in control of their situations.

God controls events that are totally out of your control.

How God's sovereignty and our free will can work together at the same time has always been a mystery, but we do know that both are involved in accomplishing His purposes. The Lord plays a part and we play a part, but His role is much larger than ours. It is like the elephant and the mouse that crossed over a rope bridge together. When they got to the other side, the mouse said, "We sure made that bridge bounce, didn't we?"

God plays the bigger role. He is running the entire universe. He controls events and circumstances that are totally out of your control. All He asks you to do is obey Him. When you learn to follow His lead, life becomes amazingly simple.

Where do you draw the line between His part and your part? If you do not know where the boundary is, you will either play the role of God by trying to run the world, or you will sit back and expect Him to do everything for you. Both extremes are wrong. You will get frustrated if you try to make something happen that only God can do. And you will miss life's adventure if you do not follow His lead.

The secret to a worry-free life is to place your trust in God and follow His guidance. If you will do what God asks of you, He will guide you down the right paths and take care of what you need.

What is God's responsibility and what is yours? The Bible draws the line for you. Each of the following verses shows God's part and your part.

Your Part (Obedience)	God's Part (Guidance and Provision)
The mind of man plans his way,	but the LORD directs his steps. (Proverbs 16:9)
I sought the LORD,	and He answered me, and delivered me from all my fears. (Psalm 34:4)
In my trouble I cried to the LORD,	and He answered me. (Psalm 120:1)
Whoever will call on the name of the Lord	will be saved. (Romans 10:13)
Trust in the LORD with all your heart, and do not rely on your own understanding; think about Him in all your ways,	and He will guide you on the right paths. (Proverbs 3:5–6 HCSB)
Seek first His kingdom and His righteousness,	and all these things [you need] will be added to you. (Matthew 6:33)
From those who walk uprightly	no good thing does He withhold. (Psalm 84:11)
Humble yourselves in the presence of the Lord,	and He will exalt you. (James 4:10)
Delight yourself in the LORD	and He will give you the desires of your heart. (Psalm 37:4)
If any of you lacks wisdom, let him ask of God . . .	and it will be given to him. (James 1:5)
Call upon Me in the day of trouble;	I shall rescue you. (Psalm 50:15)
Cast your burden upon the LORD	and He will sustain you. (Psalm 55:22)
Never take your own revenge, beloved,	but leave room for the wrath of God. (Romans 12:19)
Honor the LORD from your wealth and from the first of all your produce;	so your barns will be filled with plenty, and your vats will overflow with new wine. (Proverbs 3:9–10)
The horse is prepared for the day of battle,	but victory belongs to the LORD. (Proverbs 21:31)

The Lord wants to lead you through this life and calm all your fears and worries. In the coming chapters, you will discover the various ways God can speak to you and why you should trust Him. Once you understand that the Lord really does control the world, it will be easy for you to place your faith in Him. Trusting God is the key to experiencing a joyful life.

The next chapter contains more amazing stories of God's intervention in people's lives.

➡ LEARNING TO TRUST

1. What are some things that you learned from Pete and Robin's story?

2. Psalm 103:19 says, "The LORD has established His throne in the heavens, and His sovereignty rules over all." God does not cause evil to happen, so how can He give everyone a free will and still be in control?

3. God plays a part and you play a part in what happens. What is a word that describes the role God wants you to play?

4. Read the list of verses showing your part and God's part. How many of them are you obeying?

2

Divine Appointments

A coincidence is a small miracle where God chose
to remain anonymous.

—Heidi Quade

God promises to guide and provide for His children, but that does not mean you will never experience times when He will stretch your faith. He typically does not rush to your rescue whenever you go through a trial. Sometimes the Lord will test your faith by delaying the answer to your prayers, which forces you to wait and trust Him to come through.

At times it may seem as if God does not care about what you are going through. But just because you are not aware of His presence does not mean that He is ignoring your situation. He often provides at the last minute, when circumstances look like they could not get any worse.

Max Wilkins is the senior pastor of The Family Church in Gainesville, Florida. Shortly after he surrendered his life to go into full-time ministry, Max applied to Candler School of Theology at Emory University. He had no money to attend graduate school but took the first step of faith to get in by applying.

Max had two summer employment possibilities before fall classes would begin. The most promising opportunity was an assistant pastor position in a local church. The staff job would not only give him valuable ministry training, but the salary would completely pay for his first semester at the seminary.

The other job opportunity for the summer did not look nearly as attractive. He would be working at a church camp in the woods for 35 cents per week. The correct decision appeared to be obvious. The church staff job had to be the right choice. But after spending time in prayer, Max felt uneasy about accepting the church job. Instead, he felt God pulling at his heart to work at the camp.

His parents were shocked when he informed them that he had turned down the assistant pastor job. Like all reasonable parents, they tried to talk him out of it. "Son, you need to pray again. Obviously you didn't hear that from God."

But Max could not deny that the Lord was leading him in a direction that defied logic. It would be financially impossible for him to pay for seminary with the money he would be making. Nevertheless, he packed up his belongings and headed to camp.

For the next two and a half months, Max faithfully fulfilled his camp duties and collected his 35 cents at the end of each week. By the end of the summer, Max had earned a grand total of five dollars, and classes would be starting in two weeks.

As he thought about his pitiful financial situation, he realized that his parents had been right. Soon he would be returning home to hear them say, "We told you so." If he had listened to them in the first place and taken the other job, he would have had the money to pay for his first semester at school. But now that option was gone.

How could God let him make a huge mistake like that? Max had asked the Lord to show him which job to take and he truly believed God had pointed him to the camp. At the time he believed he had made the right decision. But now it became clear that he would not be attending fall classes in seminary. Perhaps the Lord had another path in mind.

Max stormed down to the camp lake to have it out with God. Standing by the lake, he cried out, "Lord, what are You doing to me? You are the One who called me to seminary. You are the One who called me to work at this camp. I am trying to be obedient to You, but I have no idea what to do now. This is Your problem, God!"

At that moment he sensed the presence of someone nearby. He turned around and noticed an elderly woman quietly sitting on the lakeside bench.

"Uh, hello," Max said, embarrassed about his prayer. "Have we met before?"

"No, you don't know me. My name is Emily Ann. You and I need to talk. Why don't you tell me what's bothering you."

"Well, okay, I guess."

Max sat next to her and shared about his call to ministry, his desire to attend seminary and turning down the assistant pastor job to work at the summer camp for 35 cents per week.

"Now camp is almost over and I have no money," he explained. "Seminary classes will start in two weeks. I have no idea what I am going to do with my life."

"You want to go to Candler School of Theology?" she asked. "My husband and I happen to have some friends who are endowing a scholarship at that seminary. Please give me your contact information and I will tell them about you."

Max wondered if she was making up the answer to his problem, or if she might be a little bit senile. After all, what are the odds that a person with connections to a scholarship to the very seminary he had applied for would come to that exact spot on the lakeshore at the precise time he was there praying? It made more sense to believe that she was senile and that her wealthy friend was a figment of her imagination.

Max scribbled his address on a piece of paper and handed it to her. "Well, it was nice talking with you," he remarked as he walked away.

After returning to his cabin, a friend said, "Hey Max, I have been looking for you. Where have you been?"

"I've been down at the lake, talking to a crazy woman." Max chuckled as he lay in his bed, staring at the ceiling. "She claims that she is going to try to get me a scholarship to Candler. Yeah, right!"

When summer camp ended, Max returned to his parents' home, trying to figure out his next step. A stack of mail that had accumulated over the summer was lying on his desk. As Max sorted through each piece of correspondence, he came across a letter from the Sherman Foundation. Tearing it open, he read:

Dear Max,

Our dear friend Emily Ann spoke very highly of you and your calling to ministry. We trust her implicitly. Based on her recommendation, we are pleased to award you an all-expense-paid scholarship to Candler School of Theology at Emory University.

Sincerely,
Frank and Helen Sherman
The Sherman Scholarship
Foundation

What looked like an incredibly stupid decision to work at the camp for a penny an hour turned out to be the correct decision! Because he trusted in God and followed His lead, Max did not need to worry about how the provision would be there for him. When you walk in obedience to God, He has ways of providing for you that are beyond your understanding.

The scholarship not only paid for his entire three years in seminary, but also gave him a monthly stipend for living expenses. He was able to attend seminary and concentrate on studying and ministry without having to work a part-time job.

For the last two decades, Max Wilkins has been preaching the gospel and heavily involved in foreign missions, touching many thousands of lives. None of that would have been possible if he had not made a seemingly crazy decision under God's direction—to work at a camp for 35 cents a week.[1]

> A divine appointment is when God leads someone, who usually does not know he or she is being led, to a certain place, in His perfect timing, to accomplish His specific purpose.

Max's amazing testimony shows how God can maneuver people to the right locations at the right times to accomplish His purposes. Yet this is not an isolated case. He orchestrates divine appointments every day all over the world.

A divine appointment is when God leads someone, who usually does not know he or she is being led, to a certain place, in His perfect timing, to accomplish His specific purpose. These heavenly arrangements are usually identified by four characteristics:

1. The person or persons typically are not aware that God is guiding them.
2. Their paths will cross at a certain place.

3. The timing must be precise for the two paths to intersect.
4. The encounter is for a divine purpose, which usually changes a person's destiny.

Divine appointments are often called coincidences by skeptics. However, when you consider the unbelievable odds of their occurring, it becomes abundantly clear that these perfectly timed meetings are not happening by accident. A "higher power" is arranging the circumstances and guiding the parties involved. In fact, you may have already experienced several of these divine encounters in your own life, even if you were not aware of them at the time.

> Many divine appointments occur when you least expect them, which takes the burden of trying to make them happen off of you.

How does the Lord guide you to the appointed places without your knowing about it? Sometimes He will drop an idea into your mind that you fail to recognize is coming from Him. It seems to be your own thought. You decide to go to a particular place, never realizing that He is leading you there.

His guidance is so natural, you are completely oblivious to the fact that God is directing your steps. "The mind of man plans his way, but the LORD directs his steps" (Proverbs 16:9). When you are yielded to Him, He will maneuver you from one place to another by planting ideas in your mind and desires in your heart. As you start taking those steps, He watches over you from heaven and orchestrates circumstances so that you will arrive at the correct destination at the right time. "The steps of a man are established by the LORD, and He delights in his way" (Psalm 37:23).

God can make the paths of a man and a woman intersect in His predetermined timing, which eventually leads to their marriage. If you are not married, you do not need to worry about how you will meet the right person, which will be discussed later. Many divine appointments occur when you least expect them, which takes the burden of trying to make them happen off of you.

If you will simply live to please the Lord, He will make sure that you will meet your future spouse in His timing. This will require trust and patience on your part, but it will be worth it. When everything is ready for the appointment to occur, He will make the arrangements for you two to meet.

When Moses was approaching age forty, "*it entered his mind* to visit his brethren, the sons of Israel*" (Acts 7:23). How did that thought enter his mind? The Lord planted it there because He wanted Moses to be the future leader of the Hebrew people.

> God will maneuver you from one place to another by planting ideas in your mind and desires in your heart.

Amazingly, even when people are not believers, the Lord can and does plant thoughts in their minds to accomplish His purposes. He put a prophecy into the mind of the high priest Caiaphas without his realizing it. Caiaphas said, "'It is expedient for you that one man should die for the people, and that the whole nation not perish.' Now *he did not say this on his own initiative*, but being high priest that year, he prophesied that Jesus was going to die for the nation" (John 11:50–51). Although Caiaphas did not realize that he was speaking a prophecy, the Lord put those words in his mind, which he verbalized.

King Hezekiah was afraid because the king of Assyria was planning to invade Jerusalem. The Lord said, "*I will put a spirit in him so that he shall hear a rumor* and return to his own land.

And I will make him fall by the sword in his own land" (2 Kings 19:7). God caused the Assyrian king to hear a rumor and change his mind, which kept him from capturing Jerusalem.

In another Old Testament incident, four lepers decided to go to the enemy's camp to ask for food because their city was under siege. It was a risky move that could have cost them their lives. But *"the Lord had caused the army of the Arameans to hear* a sound of chariots and a sound of horses," so that they fled and abandoned their camp. When the lepers arrived at the location, an abundance of free food was there for the taking (see 2 Kings 7:3–6). Again, God brought about a change in circumstances by inserting sounds into their minds, which they believed were the noise of horses and chariots.

Divine appointments usually are not obvious until all the pieces fit together and the dots are connected. Then we realize that God's hand was involved in making it happen, which accomplishes His specific purpose.

William P. Mackay was born in Scotland in 1839. When he left for college at seventeen years old, his mother gave him a Bible to take, writing his name in the flyleaf. After graduating from the University of Edinburgh, he enrolled in medical school. During this time, he rejected the Christian faith he had been taught growing up, so he sold the Bible his mother had given him. Mackay later became a successful doctor and was the head physician at the largest hospital in Edinburgh. He was also elected president of an atheist's society in that city.

One day a critically injured man was brought to the hospital and placed under Dr. Mackay's care. When his condition worsened, the doctor inquired if he had any relatives they could notify. The patient asked for someone to contact his landlady and tell her to bring him "the book." Within a few hours, an elderly woman arrived with the man's Bible. The man passed away shortly after that.

The man's last request for his personal Bible made Dr. Mackay curious. He flipped it open to the flyleaf and was shocked by what he saw. There, on that page, was his own name, written in his mother's penmanship! Against all odds, the Bible he had sold years before had made it back into his own hands. It was as if God had sent him a personal message to reconsider his beliefs.

He slipped the worn-out Bible under his coat and rushed back to his private office. The doctor fell to his knees, asking God to forgive him for his many years of unbelief. Here are Dr. Mackay's own words about seeing his name on the front page of the Bible:

> I took the Bible and—could I trust my eyes? It was my own Bible! The Bible which my mother had given me when I left my parents' home, and which later, when short of money, I sold for a small amount. My name was still in it, written in my mother's hand. . . . With a deep sense of shame I looked upon the precious Book. It had given comfort and refreshing to the unfortunate man in his last hours. It had been a guide to him into eternal life, so that he had been enabled to die in peace and happiness. And this book, the last gift to me from my mother, I had actually sold for a ridiculous price. . . . Be it sufficient to say that the regained possession of my Bible was the cause of my conversion.[2]

This experience made such an impact on him that the highly respected physician changed careers and became a Presbyterian minister, author and songwriter. William P. Mackay wrote seventeen hymns, including one that has been sung by millions of Christians, "Revive Us Again."[3]

Divine Appointments in Scripture

The Bible is filled with instances where God supernaturally brought people together, miraculously answered prayers just in time and fulfilled prophecies given hundreds of years before.

Divine appointments prove that God is in control, as shown in the following Scripture references. We will examine some of these in more detail in other chapters.

1. It was no coincidence that Caesar Augustus imposed a census on the entire inhabited world. This one decision set circumstances in motion for a divine appointment, which would fulfill a prophecy made centuries beforehand. Augustus's decree forced Joseph and his nine-month pregnant wife, Mary, to travel to the tiny town of Bethlehem, where she gave birth to Jesus. Out of all the cities in the world, the prophet Micah pinpointed Bethlehem as the birthplace of the Messiah seven hundred years earlier (see Micah 5:2; Luke 2:1–6).

2. Jesus asked Peter to cast a hook into the Sea of Galilee and foretold that the first fish he would catch would have a coin in its mouth to pay the temple tax. Even though thousands of fish were in the sea, God made sure the right fish was at the right place, at the right time, with the right amount. The Lord arranged for Peter to catch the only fish with a coin in its mouth (see Matthew 17:27).

3. When Joseph was thrown into the pit by his brothers, the Lord guided the Midianite traders down the correct path at just the right time to rescue him. They then transported him to Egypt so that he could fulfill God's plan (see Genesis 37:25–28).

4. When the sailors threw Jonah overboard, God guided a whale to the correct spot at the right time to catch him and take him back to shore (see Jonah 1:15–17).

5. When Abraham was about to offer up Isaac, the Lord arranged for a ram to get its horns caught in the thicket at the right place and at the exact moment to become the substitute sacrifice (see Genesis 22:10–13).

6. The arrow shot by a soldier at random had the correct direction and timing to strike wicked King Ahab in a tiny

joint in his armor, which fulfilled a prophecy by Micaiah (see 2 Chronicles 18:12–16, 33–34).

7. When Saul searched for his father's lost donkeys, he met Samuel at the appointed time which had been set by God the day before (see 1 Samuel 9:3–24).

8. At the exact moment Peter denied Jesus for the third time, a rooster near the courtyard crowed, exactly as Jesus predicted (see Matthew 26:74–75).

9. When Abraham's servant went out searching for a wife for Isaac, he traveled hundreds of miles and arrived at the right place, the city of Nahor in Mesopotamia. Rebekah just happened to go to the well at the same time as the servant prayed for God to show him the right woman. She even said the exact words the servant had requested from God as a sign, proving she was the future wife appointed for Isaac (see Genesis 24).

10. God told Gideon to sneak into the Midianites' camp and he would hear what they would say. He unknowingly went to the right tent, just in time to overhear an enemy soldier relating a dream that Gideon would defeat them. God had given the soldier the dream and prompted him to speak about it at the exact moment Gideon was eavesdropping on them (see Judges 7:9–15).

11. Pharaoh ordered all Hebrew baby boys to be killed. When Moses was three months old, his mother could no longer hide him. In an act of desperation, she put him in a tar-covered wicker basket among the reeds by the bank of the Nile River. Moments later, the Lord led Pharaoh's daughter to the same spot to find baby Moses. She had pity on him but knew she could not raise him. By an act of God's sovereignty, Pharaoh's daughter ended up paying the mother of Moses to take care of him (see Exodus 2:1–10).

12. Ruth "happened" to go to the field owned by Boaz to glean it. God set up this appointment so they would meet and get married. Ruth and Boaz are listed in the genealogy

of Jesus, proving this was not an accidental meeting (see Ruth 2:2–3; Matthew 1:5; Luke 3:32).

13. Esther was at the right place at the right time to become queen of Persia and save the Jewish people from being exterminated (see Esther 1–9).

14. An Ethiopian eunuch was reading the Scriptures in his chariot as he was traveling on the road to Gaza. Out of all the passages he could have chosen, he happened to read from Isaiah 53 about the Messiah's crucifixion. God led Philip to the same location at that exact moment so he could explain that the prophecy pertained to Jesus' dying for his sins (see Acts 8:26–39).

15. When Jesus sent His disciples into the city to prepare for the Passover, He prophesied that they would meet a man carrying a pitcher of water, who would lead them to a house. He also foretold that the owner would show them a large, furnished upper room where they would have the meal. It happened exactly as He predicted (see Mark 14:13–16).

If we examined every supernaturally orchestrated meeting in the Scriptures it would require the rest of this book. Even though we can find hundreds of these divine appointments recorded in Scripture, we must not make the mistake of thinking that they only happened "back then." God is actively at work today, supernaturally bringing people together to accomplish His purposes. He knows our needs even before we ask, and is able to prearrange the answer so that the provision arrives at precisely the right time.

Shortly after Dallas Theological Seminary was founded in 1924, it almost had to close its doors. The creditors were going to foreclose at noon on a certain day. President Lewis Chafer met with his faculty in the office, praying fervently that God would provide. One of the men, Dr. Harry Ironside, prayed,

"Lord, we know that you own the cattle on a thousand hills. Please sell some of them and send us the money."

In the meantime, a Texas businessman stepped into the seminary's business office and said, "I just sold two carloads of cattle in Fort Worth and I feel compelled to give the money to the seminary. Here's the check."

The surprised secretary took the check and knocked on the door of the prayer meeting. Dr. Chafer took it out of her hand and discovered it was for the exact amount of the debt. He turned to Dr. Ironside and said, "Harry, God sold the cattle!"[4]

How does God cause a businessman to sell his cattle and then, without knowing how much the seminary needed, lead him to donate the exact amount of money to prevent foreclosure just moments before the deadline? How can He guide two people, who do not know each other and are not aware they are being led, to meet at a certain place and eventually get married? He makes it happen through unconscious guidance.

Unconscious Guidance

Sometimes we get the idea that God cannot lead us to certain places unless we are keenly aware that He is directing us. We assume that we must have a huge door open for us, see a neon light flashing, follow a gigantic hand pointing us in the right direction or hear an audible voice from heaven. It is only then that we can believe we are on the right track.

Although the Lord may guide us in ways that are clear and obvious, He often directs our steps in inconspicuous ways through His anonymous leadership. Bob Mumford writes, "Most of God's guidance occurs when we're not even conscious of it. God knows the beginning and the end. He arranges circumstances. Sometimes we are required to take another look at where we've been in order to realize that God has been guiding us."[5]

In other words, it is not until we reflect and connect the dots that we realize God was directing our steps. He was guiding us even though we were oblivious to it.

In April 2001, a member of my church named Eugene had a cracked windshield in his minivan. The serviceman, who traveled between towns in his repair van, called Eugene and said, "I'll be in your city on Sunday at one o'clock to replace your windshield."

Eugene did not want to rush home after church, so he replied, "Rather than your coming to my house, I'll leave my car at my workplace so it will be easier for you to find." He drove his car to the parking lot at 7:20 that morning and left it there.

A bad storm was about to blow in, which would bring heavy rain, but for some strange reason Eugene decided to walk home instead of having his wife pick him up. He lived about ten blocks away from work. After he had walked a few blocks, a cold front blew in and started to spit rain.

As he was walking, he thought he heard a baby crying in the distance. He looked around but could not see where it was coming from. When he reached the next block, the cries grew louder and sounded desperate. He looked toward a nearby bowling alley, which was closed, and noticed an abandoned baby stroller about a hundred yards away, sitting behind the building.

Immediately Eugene sprinted to the stroller. Inside the carriage was a baby less than a year old that had turned blue due to the cold. He ripped off his shirt, quickly wrapped up the infant, and called 9-1-1 on his cell phone. Within minutes the police arrived at the scene and took the tiny baby girl to the hospital.

The infant was too far away from the street to be heard from inside a car driving by. Only someone walking down the street could have heard the cries. Just minutes after the police car left, a fierce rainstorm blew through with winds reaching forty miles per hour. If Eugene had not been walking down that particular street at that precise time, the baby would have died in the storm.

Police following up on the case discovered that a small boy who lived in a nearby apartment complex took the baby for a stroll and left her there.

Did God lead Eugene to that baby? Yes, He did. But *Eugene did not know he was being led.* The Lord usually arranges these divine connections without informing us about the details. God may lead you to meet someone at a particular place at a certain time without your knowledge of being led. But when you look back later, you will see God was actually leading you.

> It takes faith to believe that God is leading you when you have no proof or confirmation.

Reviewing the situation, God dropped a thought in the repairman's mind to come on Sunday. Next, the Lord slipped an idea in Eugene's mind to leave his car at work instead of at home. Finally, God changed Eugene's mind so he would walk home instead of calling for a ride. And that is how the Lord arranged a divine appointment to save the life of an infant.

One clear example of unconscious guidance is the case of Abram, whose name was later changed to Abraham. God told Abram to leave his father's house and He would lead him "to the land that I will show you" (Genesis 12:1). Even though Abram had no clue where he was going, he believed that the Lord would lead him to the right destination.

Many times when God sends you on "an adventure," you might not have any idea what will happen after you take the first step. Then you take that second step, a third step and so on, until you eventually reach your destination. It takes faith to believe that God is leading you when you have no proof or confirmation. Even though you may not understand where you are going, the Lord knows where He is taking you.

Abram packed up his belongings and "he went out, *not knowing where he was going*" (Hebrews 11:8). Can you imagine how scary that must have been for him? That is like loading all your earthly belongings in a moving truck, and then you start driving in a random direction. Your spouse nervously says, "I'm worried. Where in the world are we going?"

"I'm not sure. But I'll let you know when we get there."

This must have been how Abram's wife Sarai felt when he told her they were moving to a foreign land, but he did not know where it was!

Abram probably walked out his front door and prayed, "Where to now, Lord?"

"Abram, I want you to trust Me completely and not worry when you don't understand what I am doing. Start walking."

Abram looked in all four directions, then randomly chose a route. After traveling fifty miles, he decided to check again. "God, am I on the right track?"

No answer.

After traveling 100 miles, he prayed, "Okay, Lord, I'm trusting that You are in control and that You're leading me, even though I don't know where I'm going. You told me to leave and I obeyed, but it would be nice to hear some confirmation that I'm heading in the right direction."

Still no affirmation from heaven. He did not hear an assurance from God saying, "Yes, My son, you are exactly on the right path." Instead, Abram continued to wander on unfamiliar turf, simply traveling by faith alone.

He traveled 200 miles. Then 300 miles. When he hit the 450-mile marker, God finally announced, "To your descendants I will give this land" (Genesis 12:7).

God was guiding his every step even though Abram was not sure where he was going. Although Abram did not know it at the time, the entire future of the nation of Israel depended on his arriving at the right location for the Lord's people to establish themselves. This was the land where the Temple would be built and the Messiah would be born. The place where God had led him was the Promised Land!

What can we learn from this? Simply that the Lord is in control and can lead you to the right places, even when you are not conscious of His guidance. And there is no need to worry if you are placing your complete trust in God.

Perhaps you are wondering if God can guide you to your own land of promise. The answer is yes. He has a plan for your life and wants to lead you, one step at a time. The journey begins the moment you place your life in His hands.

➡ LEARNING TO TRUST

1. What lessons did you learn from Max Wilkins's story?

2. What are the four characteristics of a divine appointment? Can you think of a divine appointment in your own life?

3. How do the fifteen examples of divine appointments in Scripture show that God is in control? How does this help you to trust God and not worry?

4. God told Abram to leave his country and that He would lead him "to the land that I will show you." Why do you think God would not tell him where he was going?

3

Indisputable Proof
God Controls the World

Only the supernatural mind can have prior knowledge. If then the Bible has foreknowledge, historical
and scientific, beyond the permutation of chance, it
truly then bears the fingerprint of God.

—G. B. Hardy

We are staking everything we believe on a God who is invisible
to us. Is it too much to ask for a little proof that the Bible is
true and that He really is in control of the world? If it can be
proven that the Lord is in control, it would do wonders for our
faith and would keep us from worrying.

Your wish has been granted. God has provided indisputable
proof that He is ruling and overruling the events happening
on earth. The evidence is found in the numerous predictions
recorded in the Scriptures by the biblical prophets.

In the movie *Back to the Future Part II*, Marty McFly gets in his time machine and travels thirty years into the future. As Marty walks down the street, he notices a sports almanac displayed in an antique store window, which lists all the scores from 1950 to the year 2000. Marty buys it, intending to take the book back to 1985 so he can bet on all the games. Since the outcome of every game has already been determined in history future, he would win every time. The plan backfires when his archenemy, Biff Tannen, steals the book and places the sure bets, making himself extremely rich instead of Marty.

What if someone could come back from the future and tell us the important things that we needed to know? Such information would be priceless. It would help us tremendously to know how to plan for the future, but only if we believed the person's claims. In a very real sense, we would be "placing our bets" on whether the person from the future was being truthful or making it up.

When it comes to the claims in the Bible, everyone is placing a bet. We are betting our eternal souls that it is either true or not true, and you will either be right or wrong. It never ceases to amaze me that most people will never take the time to verify the validity of the Bible. Verification does not mean you must have your every question answered before you can believe. It simply means that you have carefully examined the evidence and have reached a final conclusion so that you can place your bet. A jury does not need to have every question answered, but it must be convinced beyond a reasonable doubt.

The prophecies of the Bible can be compared to the sports almanac that Marty bought. Just as the scores of future games were recorded in his almanac, God's predictions of future events are recorded in the Scriptures. I am not talking about the end-of-the-world prophecies that are still waiting to be fulfilled, but the predictions made by the Old Testament prophets that *have already* come to pass. The proof is not found by looking into the future, but by looking back on history. Bible prophecies that have already been fulfilled provide indisputable proof that God controls earthly events and the Bible is true.

God made many predictions in the Scriptures about future events which eventually came to pass exactly as they were recorded. On several occasions, Jesus prophesied to His disciples about His own crucifixion and resurrection so they would believe after it came to pass. He said, "I am telling you before it comes to pass, *so that when it does occur, you may believe* that I am He" (John 13:19; see also 14:29). According to the Lord Jesus, the fulfillment of prophecies gives us a solid foundation for our faith. It proves that God knows the future and is controlling the events that will make them come to pass.

How is it possible for anyone to predict the future when it has not yet occurred? The prophets claimed they received their information directly from God, who told them what would happen in the future. He revealed specific future details to these prophets, who recorded His words in

> Bible prophecies that have already been fulfilled provide indisputable proof that God controls earthly events and the Bible is true.

the Scriptures. Each prediction of the future is called a prophecy, and the Bible records hundreds of prophecies.

The prophets would die long before most of their predictions would come to pass. They would never see the fulfillment during their lifetimes. God told them that their prophecies were intended for the future generations to examine:

> As to this salvation, the prophets who prophesied of the grace that would come to you made careful searches and inquiries, seeking to know what person or time the Spirit of Christ within

them was indicating as He predicted the sufferings of Christ and the glories to follow. *It was revealed to them that they were not serving themselves, but you,* in these things which now have been announced to you through those who preached the gospel to you by the Holy Spirit.

1 Peter 1:10–12

This passage reveals that the prophets were curious about when their prophecies would come to pass. The Lord told them that the events they predicted would be fulfilled at a much later time and that future generations would be examining their prophecies. Only time would tell if these prophets truly were God's spokespersons or just crazy fanatics who were trying to draw attention to themselves.

Time has proven the prophets to be correct. Today, thanks to the meticulous work of scribes who carefully copied and preserved their predictions, we can look back on history and see that their prophecies were fulfilled exactly as they had proclaimed.

Take a moment and think this through. For a prophecy to be made and fulfilled, seven things need to take place.

Seven Factors Necessary for a Prophecy to Be Fulfilled

1. *God must know everything that will happen in the future*

For God to predict the future, He would need foreknowledge of the coming events. The Lord can see everything that happens throughout all time and can therefore predict the future. "I am God, and there is no one like Me, *declaring the end from the beginning, and from ancient times things which have not been done*, saying, 'My purpose will be established, and I will accomplish all My good pleasure'" (Isaiah 46:9–10). When God says that His purpose will be established, it means that He is actively involved in making His plan come to pass.

2. God must communicate His message to a spokesperson on earth, a prophet

Peter said, "The things which *God announced beforehand by the mouth of all the prophets,* that His Christ would suffer, He has thus fulfilled" and *"God spoke by the mouth of His holy prophets* from ancient time" (Acts 3:18, 21). The prophets claimed to be God's spokespersons and usually began their messages by saying, "Thus says the Lord."

3. The prophet must record God's predictions in a manuscript so that future generations would be able to verify the fulfillment

Their prophecies were recorded in the manuscripts that were compiled as the Bible. Most prophecies are clearly understood, while others are written in cryptic language. However, even the symbolic prophecies of Daniel were literally fulfilled and were understood after they came to pass.

4. God must make sure the prophetic Scriptures are copied and preserved from generation to generation for hundreds of years until the prophecy is fulfilled

Since they had no photocopiers or printing presses, the manuscripts had to be copied by hand. This task was done by scribes, who patiently copied the Scriptures when the scrolls became too worn to be used any longer.

The Jewish scribes valued the Scriptures so much that they counted every letter on each page they copied. To ensure accuracy, certain rules had to be followed. The scribes could only copy one letter at a time and not an entire word. The middle letter of the manuscript was marked, as was the middle word of each major section of a book. After a page was copied, another person counted the number of letters on that page and compared it with the original. A third person checked for the middle word on the page. If the number of letters did not match the original, they destroyed the entire page and started over.

Imagine how slowly and carefully they worked to make sure there were no mistakes. The Bible we have today would not be in existence if the scribes over many centuries had not spent countless hours duplicating the manuscripts by hand.

> The Bible we have today would not be in existence if the scribes over many centuries had not spent countless hours duplicating the manuscripts by hand.

To understand how difficult this task was, just try copying one page of the Bible without making any mistakes. If you mess up one letter, you must start over. Now think about hand copying several books of the Bible and you will get an idea of what it was like.

By the time Jesus was born, the most recent Old Testament book, Malachi, had been copied and recopied over a span of more than four hundred years. The books of Moses had been copied for more than fourteen hundred years!

5. God must make sure that people and events come together at the right time so that the prophecy comes to pass

When the prophets made their predictions, they usually did not know when their words would come to pass. Sometimes they prophesied concerning their current situations, while at other times they spoke of events that would take place in future centuries. Many of their prophecies pertained to generations yet to be born (see 1 Peter 1:10–12). Only God could control the people, events and timing so that the prophecies that were written hundreds of years beforehand would come to pass.

6. Another prophet must recognize when an Old Testament prophecy was fulfilled and record the fulfillment in the New Testament for future generations to read

When we read the gospels and other New Testament books, we notice the authors saying repeatedly, "That the Scripture might be fulfilled." Each incident refers to a prophecy made by one of the Old Testament prophets, who had predicted that particular future event. When Jesus was arrested in the Garden of Gethsemane, He said, "How then will the Scriptures be fulfilled, which say that it must happen this way? . . . But all this has taken place to fulfill the Scriptures of the prophets" (Matthew 26:54, 56). Jesus recognized the prophecy being fulfilled, which was recorded by Matthew in his gospel.

7. God must preserve the record of both the prophecy and the fulfillment so that future generations can look back on both to verify them

The Scriptures have been preserved for thousands of years. Now we can look back at the numerous prophecies made by the prophets, along with the fulfillments of those prophecies which came to pass many centuries later.

These seven factors are only possible if an eternal God is overseeing the process. This makes the study of fulfilled Bible prophecies fascinating. It is extraordinary for even one prophecy to make it through all seven steps. But to think of *hundreds* of prophecies in the Old Testament going through all seven steps is nothing short of mind-boggling! This gives us proof that the Bible is inspired by God and we can therefore trust what it says.

Biblical Prophecies of the Future

Daniel 4:25 says, "The Most High is ruler over the realm of mankind." Since God controls the world, it is no problem for Him to predict what will happen in the future and communicate this information to the prophets. Forget about Nostradamus. He could not hold a candle to the Old Testament prophets.

The prophet **Daniel** gave some amazing details about how the future would unfold. When I was in college, I read a book called *Daniel's Prophecy of the 70 Weeks*, which convinced me the Bible is true. In his prophecy, Daniel prophesied both the first and second comings of Christ (see Daniel 9:24–27). He described what some have called a "prophetic time clock" of 490 years (the Jewish "week" being seven years, not seven days), which would pinpoint the exact day when the Messiah would be revealed.

Daniel prophesied that when a decree went forth to restore and rebuild Jerusalem, the clock would start counting down. That decree was issued by King Artaxerxes. Four hundred eighty-three years later, the Messiah would be revealed. Jesus fulfilled this prophecy when He rode into Jerusalem on a donkey as the crowds hailed Him as the Messiah.[1]

The prophetic clock stopped ticking when Christ was revealed the first time, which would be followed by two events. After the Messiah is revealed, Daniel further prophesied that He "will be cut off and have nothing," a clear reference to His crucifixion. Then Jerusalem and the temple would be destroyed, which was fulfilled by the Romans led by commander Titus Vespasianus in AD 70 (see Daniel 9:26). The prophet Daniel predicted this important event over six hundred years before it happened.

The seventieth week, or the final seven years, will begin when the future antichrist confirms a covenant with Israel (see Daniel 9:27). On that day, the prophetic clock will start ticking again, which culminates with the Messiah being revealed to Israel again at the Second Coming. The book of Revelation is an elaboration on Daniel's seventieth week, or the last seven years on earth before Christ returns.

The book of Daniel prophesies many other events as well. He also predicted that four world empires would successively arise over the span of hundreds of years—Babylon, then Medo-Persia, followed by Greece and finally Rome (see Daniel 2:31–45; 7:1–28). In Daniel 11:2–4, he predicted that a future king of Greece would die and his kingdom would be divided into four regions. Daniel made this prophecy in 539 BC and it was fulfilled over two hundred years later. When Alexander the Great died in 323 BC, his empire was divided among his four generals, exactly as the Scriptures predicted.

In Daniel 11:29–31, he predicted a king would arise and desecrate the temple in Jerusalem. This was fulfilled when Antiochus Epiphanes slaughtered a pig on the altar of the Jewish temple and erected an altar to the god Zeus in 168 BC. Many of the other prophecies of Daniel deal with end-time events still in the future.

The prophet **Micah** lived over seven hundred years before Christ. God communicated a specific future event to this prophet, which was recorded in the Hebrew Bible:

> But as for you, Bethlehem Ephrathah, too little to be among the clans of Judah, from you One will go forth for Me to be ruler in Israel. His goings forth are from long ago, from the days of eternity.
>
> Micah 5:2

This amazing prophecy pinpoints the birthplace of the future Messiah. Out of all the cities in the world, Micah predicted that Bethlehem would be the location where God would be born in a human body. This prophecy also defines the dual nature of Christ—as both human and divine. The Messiah would take on a physical body, but the prophecy explains that He preexisted from eternity past.

Centuries passed without the prophecy being fulfilled. Then, approximately 720 years later, events began to unfold to bring it to pass. Caesar Augustus issued a decree to tax everyone living under the Roman government. This required that everyone in Israel must return to his or her own city to register. Caesar did not realize that his order was the first step in a divine appointment.

Joseph and Mary lived in Nazareth, but both were from the house of David, which meant that they had to go back to the city of their family, which was Bethlehem. What were the odds that they would arrive in the town at the exact time Mary gave birth to Jesus, which fulfilled Micah's prophecy from seven centuries before? Only God could make that happen.

In **Zechariah** 9:9, the prophet, who lived about five hundred years before Christ, predicted that Israel's king would humbly ride into Jerusalem on a donkey. In those days, kings proudly rode on white horses through a city, but never on a donkey. Jesus fulfilled this prophecy when He rode into Jerusalem on Palm Sunday (see Luke 19:35–38). Zechariah predicted the Messiah would be betrayed for thirty pieces of silver, which was fulfilled when Judas betrayed Jesus. The prophet accurately described the exact number of pieces (thirty, not twenty-nine) and that the money would be of silver, not gold. He foretold that the money would be thrown in the sanctuary (not somewhere else), and used to buy a potter's field (see Zechariah 11:12–13; Matthew 27:3–7). He also prophesied that the disciples would forsake the Messiah (see Zechariah 13:7; Matthew 26:31, 56) and that He would be pierced, which was fulfilled when the soldiers pierced Jesus' side with a spear (see Zechariah 12:10; John 19:34).

The prophet **Isaiah**, writing seven hundred years before Christ, predicted the Messiah would be born of a virgin and would be called Immanuel, which is translated "God with us" (see Isaiah 7:14; Matthew 1:23). Chapter 53 of Isaiah paints a graphic description of the Messiah being scourged (see Isaiah 53:5; John 19:1), crucified, paying for the sins of the world and buried in a rich man's tomb (see Isaiah 53:9; Matthew 27:60). Isaiah prophesied that Jerusalem and the temple would be rebuilt, which was fulfilled two hundred years later. He even mentions a future king, Cyrus, by name one hundred fifty years before he was even born (see Isaiah 44:28; 45:1).

In Psalm 22, a thousand years before Christ was born, King David described the crucifixion of Jesus, saying that His hands and feet would be pierced (see Psalm 22:16; Luke 24:39), including the fact that they would cast lots for His garments, which was fulfilled when the soldiers cast lots for His outer garments and tunic (see Psalm 22:18; John 19:23–24). David also predicted that the Messiah would be betrayed by a friend (see Psalm 41:9; John 13:18), not a bone would be broken (see Psalm 34:20; John 19:36) and He would rise from the dead (see Psalm 16:10; Acts 2:31–32).

In a subtle way, Jesus prophesied that the New Testament would be written. When Mary anointed Him with the vial of costly perfume, He said, "Truly I say to you, wherever the gospel is preached in the whole world, what this woman has done will also be spoken of in memory of her" (Mark 14:9). I am sure Judas rolled his eyes when Jesus made that statement. He was probably thinking, *Mary's anointing Him will be made known throughout the whole world? That's impossible!* It certainly seemed ludicrous at that time, but now we see that the incident was recorded in the Bible, which has been read by millions of people all over the world.

We have not begun to scratch the surface of all the biblical prophecies and their fulfillments. Since God predicted

> If God can control global events, then you can trust Him to handle everything in your life as well.

all the above future events through His prophets and brought each one to pass, it means He is in control of the world. He can only foretell an event if He has control over it.

The fulfillment of each prophecy tells us that God oversaw the people and circumstances so that everything came together at just the right time. The fact that hundreds of Bible prophecies have been fulfilled exactly as foretold is irrefutable evidence that God not only exists, but that He is controlling history!

What does this mean to us? It means that if God can control global events, then you can trust Him to handle everything in your life as well. The same God who accurately prophesied those events also told you to not worry. You can pray to Him for guidance and provision, and He will hear you.

Imagine, the Supreme Being who holds the universe in His hand also wants to talk with you and guide you through life! If you are willing to follow Him, He will show you what to do. God's guidance and provision hinges on the fact that He controls the world.

The ancient biblical prophecies and their fulfillment give us confidence that God controls the future. The prophecies listed below were made hundreds of years before Jesus was born and were fulfilled as foretold.

Proof the Bible is True

Prophecies in the Old Testament about the Messiah	Approximate date prophesied	Fulfillment in the New Testament
He would be born of a virgin (Isaiah 7:14)	740–680 BC	Matthew 1:18–25
He would be the Son of God (Psalm 2:7)	1,000 BC	Matthew 3:17
He would be a descendant of Abraham (Genesis 12:3; 22:18)	1,400 BC	Matthew 1:1
The Messiah would be a descendant of Isaac (Genesis 21:12)	1,400 BC	Matthew 1:2; Luke 3:34

Prophecies in the Old Testament about the Messiah	Approximate date prophesied	Fulfillment in the New Testament
The Messiah would be a descendant of Jacob (Numbers 24:17)	1,400 BC	Matthew 1:2; Luke 3:34
He would be from the tribe of Judah (Genesis 49:10)	1,400 BC	Matthew 1:2; Luke 3:33
He would be from the family of Jesse (Isaiah 11:1)	740–680 BC	Matthew 1:6; Luke 3:32
The Messiah would be from the house of David (Jeremiah 23:5)	627–580 BC	Matthew 1:1; Luke 3:31
He would be raised up as a prophet like Moses (Deuteronomy 18:15, 18)	1,400 BC	Acts 3:22; 7:37
The Messiah would be born in Bethlehem (Micah 5:2)	722 BC	Matthew 2:1
After He was born, babies would be killed in Bethlehem (Jeremiah 31:15)	627–580 BC	Matthew 2:16–18
He would be called Immanuel, meaning "God with us" (Isaiah 7:14)	740–680 BC	Matthew 1:23
He would be called out of Egypt (Hosea 11:1; Joseph and Mary fled to Egypt with Jesus)	720 BC	Matthew 2:15
The Messiah would come from Galilee (Isaiah 9:1–2)	740–680 BC	Matthew 4:13–16
The Spirit of the Lord would be upon Him (Isaiah 61:1)	740–680 BC	Luke 4:16–21; Matthew 12:17–18
He would be preceded by a messenger (Malachi 3:1)	430 BC	Matthew 11:10
He would do miracles (Isaiah 35:5–6)	740–680 BC	Matthew 11:2–5
Israel's king would ride into Jerusalem on a donkey (Zechariah 9:9)	470 BC	Matthew 21:5–9; John 12:14–15
The Messiah would be welcomed with "Blessed is He who comes in the name of the Lord" (Psalm 118:26)	1,000 BC	John 12:13

Prophecies in the Old Testament about the Messiah	Approximate date prophesied	Fulfillment in the New Testament
He would be hated for no reason (Psalm 35:19; 69:4)	1,000 BC	John 15:25
He would be rejected by the religious rulers (Psalm 118:22)	1,000 BC	Matthew 21:42
He would be rejected by His own brothers (Psalm 69:8)	1,000 BC	John 7:5
He would be betrayed by a friend (Psalm 41:9)	1,000 BC	Matthew 10:4
His betrayer would eat bread with Him (Psalm 41:9)	1,000 BC	John 13:18, 26; Mark 14:18
He would be betrayed for 30 pieces of silver (Zechariah 11:12)	470 BC	Matthew 26:15
The money would be returned (Zechariah 11:12–13)	470 BC	Matthew 27:3
The money would be thrown in the house of the Lord (Zechariah 11:13)	470 BC	Matthew 27:5
The betrayal money would pay for a potter's field (Zechariah 11:13)	470 BC	Matthew 27:7
He would be forsaken by the disciples (Zechariah 13:7)	470 BC	Matthew 26:31, 56
He would be silent before His accusers (Isaiah 53:7)	740–680 BC	Matthew 26:62–63
The Messiah would be mocked (Isaiah 53:3)	740–680 BC	Matthew 27:29
He would be beaten with a rod (Micah 5:1)	722 BC	Mark 15:19
He would be spat upon in the face (Isaiah 50:6)	740–680 BC	Mark 14:65
The Messiah would be wounded, bruised (Isaiah 53:5)	740–680 BC	Matthew 27:30; Luke 22:63
The Messiah would be scourged on His back (Isaiah 50:6, 53:5)	740–680 BC	John 19:1

Prophecies in the Old Testament about the Messiah	Approximate date prophesied	Fulfillment in the New Testament
His hands and feet would be pierced (Psalm 22:16)	1,000 BC	John 20:25
His garments would be divided (Psalm 22:18)	1,000 BC	John 19:23
They would cast lots for His clothing (Psalm 22:18)	1,000 BC	John 19:24
The Messiah would die with criminals (Isaiah 53:12)	740–680 BC	Mark 15:28; Luke 22:37
Those watching the crucifixion would wag their heads (Psalm 22:7; 109:25)	1,000 BC	Mark 15:29; Matthew 27:39
Those watching the crucifixion would mock Him for not saving Himself (Psalm 22:8)	1,000 BC	Matthew 27:41–43
He would pray for those crucifying Him (Isaiah 53:12)	740–680 BC	Luke 23:34
He would be given vinegar to drink (Psalm 69:21)	1,000 BC	Matthew 27:34
"Why hast thou forsaken me?" (Psalm 22:1 kjv)	1,000 BC	Matthew 27:46
"Into thine hand I commit my spirit" (Psalm 31:5 kjv)	1,000 BC	Luke 23:46
His side would be pierced (Zechariah 12:10)	470 BC	John 19:34, 37
None of the Messiah's bones would be broken (Psalm 34:20)	1,000 BC	John 19:32–36
He would be buried in a rich man's tomb (Isaiah 53:9)	740–680 BC	Matthew 27:57–60
He would be dead for three days and three nights (Jonah 1:17)	760 BC	Matthew 12:40
He would descend into hell (Psalm 16:10; 49:15)	1,000 BC	Acts 2:27, 31; Ephesians 4:9
The Messiah would be resurrected from the dead (Psalm 16:10; 30:3)	1,000 BC	Acts 2:31; 13:33–35

Prophecies in the Old Testament about the Messiah	Approximate date prophesied	Fulfillment in the New Testament
Through His resurrection He would swallow up death in victory (Isaiah 25:8)	740–680 BC	1 Corinthians 15:54
He would ascend into heaven (Psalm 68:18)	1,000 BC	Acts 1:9; Ephesians 4:8–10
He would be seated at the right hand of the Father in heaven (Psalm 110:1)	1,000 BC	Acts 2:34–35; Colossians 3:1
He would be a priest according to the order of Melchizedek (Psalm 110:4)	1,000 BC	Hebrews 5:6, 10; 6:20
The Messiah would be a light to the entire world, including non-Jews (Isaiah 42:6; 49:6)	740–680 BC	Luke 2:32; Acts 13:47; 26:23

Jesus fulfilled more than three hundred prophecies in the Bible. Peter Stoner in *Science Speaks* calculated the probability of one man fulfilling 48 prophecies to be 1 in 10 to the 157th power.[2]

1 in 10,000, 000, 000, 000, 000, 000, 000, 000, 000, 000, 000, 000, 000, 000, 000, 000, 000, 000, 000, 000, 000, 000, 000, 000, 000, 000, 000, 000, 000, 000, 000, 000, 000, 000, 000, 000, 000, 000, 000, 000, 000, 000, 000, 000, 000, 000, 000, 000, 000, 000, 000, 000, 000

Now do you believe that God is in control? Only a supernatural God could have inspired and fulfilled the prophecies in the Bible. The evidence is so compelling that it should convince you beyond a reasonable doubt. God's fingerprints are all over it!

Don't you think that the God who brought all these circumstances together can handle the situations that worry you? Once you grasp the fact that the Lord has the ability to control circumstances, it becomes much easier to place your trust in Him. Now let's take a closer look at the amazing knowledge of God.

➡ LEARNING TO TRUST

1. God told His prophets to record predictions of certain events that would take place in the future. What was the purpose of this? (See John 13:19 and 14:29.)

2. The scribes over the centuries realized the importance of the Scriptures and carefully copied the manuscripts by hand. We would not have the Bible today without their meticulous work. What can we do today to make sure their work was not in vain?

3. What do fulfilled Bible prophecies teach us about God's foreknowledge and power? How does this apply to our own problems that we worry about?

4. What does Peter Stoner's calculation about probabilities prove to us about the inspiration of God's Word?

5. Since the Old Testament prophecies concerning Christ were fulfilled with 100 percent accuracy, what can we conclude about the promises God has made to us in His Word?

4

God's IQ

Bring me a worm that can comprehend a man, and then I will show you a man that can comprehend the triune God.

—John Wesley

Mirror, mirror on the wall, who is the smartest one of all? Good question. Here is a list of some of the highest IQs.

Kim Ung-yong, physicist and engineer, 210

Sir Isaac Newton, physicist, 190

Garry Kasparov, world chess champion, 190

Marilyn Vos Savant, author, 186 (one test measured her IQ at 228)[1]

Benjamin Netanyahu, Prime Minister of Israel, 180

Blaise Pascal, physicist, 171

Andrew Wiles, mathematician, 170

Judith Polgar, world chess champion, 170
Robert Byrne, chess grandmaster, 170
Bobby Fischer, world chess champion, 167
Stephen W. Hawking, physicist, over 160
Albert Einstein, physicist, 160[2]

After reviewing that list, I have concluded that if I am ever going to raise my IQ, I will need to either become a part-time physicist or take up chess.

To place your complete trust in God, you must not only believe that He controls the world, but that He also knows all things. How could you adequately assign an IQ to someone who knows *everything*?

Even so, many people think they are smarter than God, and that is why they live the way they do. Others believe in God but have never given much thought to His omniscience—that He is all-knowing. They believe the purpose of prayer is to inform Him about what is happening in their lives. If they do not tell Him, He will never know.

Trust comes from placing your confidence in another person. You trust your doctor because you believe she knows how to diagnose your problem and prescribe the correct medicine. You trust your mechanic because you believe he knows how to repair your vehicle and will not rip you off. You trust God because you believe that He knows everything about your situation and will somehow make everything work out for your good—even when it does not look like it at the time. Trusting God with your life is the cure for worry.

There is an old story about four blind men who were trying to describe an elephant. The first grabbed the elephant's leg and said, "An elephant is like a tree trunk." The second blind man grabbed its tail, saying, "No, it's not. An elephant is like a rope." The third man grabbed its ear. "No, an elephant is like a big leaf." The fourth man grabbed its trunk and argued, "You are all wrong. An elephant is like a fire hose." They were all partially correct, but they were also all wrong because none of them had the complete picture.

To place your trust in God, you must understand His entire character and not just focus on one attribute. The *heart* of God is His compassion—His love for all people. The *hand* of God is His omnipotence—His power over all things. The *mind* of God is His omniscience—His knowledge of all things.

Because God knows all things, He can see the outcome of every possible scenario that could take place in the future. He understands what would happen if you took route A and the outcome if you chose route B, C, or Z. When you surrender yourself completely to His leadership, He will guide you down the right path in life. The Lord sees and understands things that you do not have the ability to comprehend.

I once had a dog that had an IQ of 1, maybe 2. If I had read Bandit every book in my library trying to educate him, it would have been a waste of time. Bandit was not capable of understanding human thinking because "people thoughts" are higher than "dog thoughts." Just as people are much smarter than dogs, God is more intelligent than any human. His thoughts are infinitely higher than ours:

> "For My thoughts are not your thoughts, nor are your ways My ways," declares the Lord. "For as the heavens are higher than the earth, so are My ways higher than your ways and My thoughts than your thoughts."
>
> Isaiah 55:8–9

The **heart** of God is His compassion.

The **hand** of God is His omnipotence.

The **mind** of God is His omniscience.

No one on this earth has ever been able to comprehend how incredibly intelligent God is. Consider how your life would improve if you would always follow His advice. Since God always knows the best path for you to take, He is able to guide you down the road where you will be the most fulfilled. He has already revealed in His Word that He wants to lead you, but you must be willing to follow. The Lord promised to guide King David in his decisions: "I will instruct you and teach you in the way which you should go; I will counsel you with My eye upon you" (Psalm 32:8).

God told the prophet Jeremiah, "Thus says the LORD who made the earth . . . 'Call to Me and I will answer you, and I will tell you great and mighty things, which you do not know'" (Jeremiah 33:2–3). The amount of information He will share with you is at His own discretion. He will not tell you everything, but He will reveal those things that you need to know at that moment—to help you make right decisions.

What Does God Know?

To even begin to grasp God's intelligence, we must examine what the Bible reveals about His knowledge of all things. Let's begin with the big picture and then work our way down to the little details.

1. God knows the number of stars and gives them all names

Consider the vastness of the universe. Astronomers estimate we have approximately 100 thousand million stars in the Milky Way alone.[3] And that is just in one galaxy! Add to that the number of stars in the millions of other galaxies. Astronomers calculate the number of stars in the known universe to be 300 sextillion. That is 300,000 million million million or 3 followed by 23 zeroes.[4] There are ten times as many stars as grains of sand on all the world's beaches and deserts.[5]

Why in the world (or maybe we should say universe) did God create so many stars? It seems like a colossal waste of power just to decorate the sky. But think about it. If God wanted to demonstrate His royal majesty and unmatched power, how would He do it? He would create something so enormous that it would blow our minds, such as millions of galaxies.

The Creator is so powerful that speaking the universe into existence was no big deal for Him. All He had to do was just whisper a word. When we observe the staggering numbers of stars, we are utterly amazed as we consider how powerful this Intelligent Designer must be. This is exactly why He crafted the heavenly expanse, as is confirmed in this passage: "The heavens are telling of the glory of God; and their expanse is declaring the work of His hands" (Psalm 19:1).

And not only did He create the stars, but He also assigned a name to each one:

Lift up your eyes on high and see who has created these stars, the One who leads forth their host by number, *He calls them all by name*; because of the greatness of His might and the strength of His power, not one of them is missing.

Isaiah 40:26

He counts the number of the stars; *He gives names to all of them*. Great is our Lord and abundant in strength; His understanding is infinite.

Psalm 147:4–5

Why did God give a name to each star? Are any stars named Fred or Wilma? Just as parents name their children, the Creator assigned an appropriate title to everything He created. Not only did He make them, but He also sustains each one through His power.

2. God numbers the hairs of each person in the entire world

Now that we have used the telescope to examine the enormity of the universe, we need to turn our attention in the opposite direction and peep through the microscope. Why would the Creator who spoke all the galaxies into existence be concerned with the small stuff? It is because He takes personal interest in everything He created—including you.

Noted English Bible preacher G. Campbell Morgan said, "God is in the infinitely little as well as in the infinitely great." Jesus made an astounding announcement that no doubt dropped the jaws of every one of His listeners. He revealed that the Father knows the smallest details of our lives when He said, "Indeed, the very *hairs of your head are all numbered*" (Luke 12:7).

Although the number of hairs on a person's head varies from one individual to another, the average is about 100,000. The quantity varies according to gender, age, race, hair color and genetic makeup.[6] Most people shed about 100 hairs a day, and since the citizenship of the world increases by approximately 200,000 each day, the total number of hairs on the planet is in constant fluctuation.

The world's population is approximately 6.7 billion. If we multiply that number by 100,000 hairs, we find that God is keeping track of 670 trillion hairs on people's heads. And that is not counting the beards.

We would never have known this amazing fact about God's knowledge if Jesus had not revealed it to us. God wants us to know how much He knows. Imagine, this Divine Being knows even the smallest of details about you and me, down to each hair!

With all the problems in the world, why would God waste His time counting hairs? Actually, He is not counting. He just knows—and that is the point. Jesus often shocked His audiences by teaching about things that were humanly impossible, like camels going through the eye of a needle, or casting mountains into the sea by faith. He used "shock treatments" to jolt His listeners out of the prison of logic so they would think outside the box.

If God knows the exact number of hairs on your head, it proves that He is also aware of every other detail about you as well. Keep this fact in mind because your faith will grow as you begin to grasp the infinite power and knowledge of the God who loves you.

Jesus added another astonishing statement to reveal God's knowledge: "Are not two sparrows sold for a cent? And yet not one of them will fall to the ground apart from your Father" (Matthew 10:29). God knows where every sparrow in the entire world is right now. Not a single one can fall to the ground without His notice.

We have no way of monitoring or keeping track of the number of sparrows in our city, much less the world. How could anyone even begin to do that? Certainly billions of birds are fluttering about the planet at this very moment. They are hiding in bushes and flying from tree to tree, yet the Lord knows where each one is.

> Jesus used "shock treatments" to jolt His listeners out of the prison of logic so they would think outside the box.

God cares for the least valuable of all the birds (sold for a half cent each), and that means He is more concerned about you because you are of eternal worth. Jesus said, "So do not fear; you are more valuable than many sparrows" (Matthew 10:31).

Seventy sextillion stars—and the Lord has a name for each one.

Six hundred seventy trillion hairs—and God numbers each one.

Billions of birds constantly on the move—and He monitors each one.

What else does He know?

3. God reads the thoughts of every person in the world

Have you ever thought about what a "thought" is? It is an idea inside your mind, but what is it really? No one has ever seen a thought before. Yet God not only knows what you are thinking, but also what everyone else in the world is thinking. Scripture tells us the Lord does read minds. "The LORD knows the thoughts of man" (Psalm 94:11).

Okay, now this is really getting creepy. I can see you squirming right now. You would like to keep some of your thoughts to yourself, right?

But isn't it comforting to know that God understands exactly what you are going through? He is intimately acquainted with your hurts. He can actually feel your pain. And since He can read your mind, you can communicate with Him both through your thoughts and your words.

One day Jesus' disciples got into an argument among themselves concerning who was the greatest. They could not hide their squabble from Jesus because He had been reading their minds all along. "But Jesus, *knowing what they were thinking* in their heart, took a child and stood him by His side" (Luke 9:47). Using a child as an example of humility, He explained that the least among them was actually the greatest.

When Jesus healed a paralytic man and forgave his sins, "Some of the scribes said to themselves, 'This fellow blasphemes.' And Jesus *knowing their thoughts* said, 'Why are you thinking evil in your hearts?'" (Matthew 9:3–4). He had been reading their minds, proving He also had the power to forgive sins.

King David was keenly aware of what God knew. He wrote:

You know when I sit down and when I rise up; *You understand my thought* from afar. You scrutinize my path and my lying down, and are intimately acquainted with all my ways. Even before there is a word on my tongue, behold, O LORD, *You know it all. . . .* Such knowledge is too wonderful for me; It is too high, I cannot attain to it.

Psalm 139:2–4, 6

Now, do you really believe that God does not know what is going on in your life? He knows every time you sit down and every time you stand up. He is aware of the exact moment you open the door and turn the ignition key in your car. He knows every word you say, even before you speak it.

David said such knowledge was "too wonderful" and "too high" for him to grasp. How is it possible for God to know every thought and every word of every person in every nation every second of every day? Yet He does.

The biblical prophets had an uncanny ability to hear the Lord's voice with great clarity. God spoke to the prophet Elisha about the king of Aram in such detail that the king's servant told him, "Elisha, the prophet who is in Israel, tells the king of Israel *the words that you speak in your bedroom*" (2 Kings 6:12). Such knowledge is so far beyond our comprehension that our minds would experience a meltdown trying to figure it out. God's knowledge is in a league of its own—a totally different realm of knowledge.

Trying to contact God through our intelligence is such an impossible task that it would require a shortcut, like the theoretical wormhole that cuts through space and time. We do not have enough lifetimes to travel across the universe collecting enough data and information to get on His level. We need another way to understand God, who He is and what He wants. The theological wormhole that takes us directly to God is called "faith."

Now we understand why Jesus said, "I praise You, O Father, Lord of heaven and earth, that You have hidden these things from the wise and intelligent and have revealed them to infants. Yes, Father, for this way was well-pleasing in Your sight" (Luke 10:21).

Did Jesus just say that God *hides* things from the wise and intelligent? Yes, He did. Some highly intelligent people have concluded God does not exist because they have failed to discover Him with their minds. They will never find Him unless they start looking with the spiritual part of their being.

God created everyone with different levels of intelligence. If knowledge was the correct avenue needed to connect with Him, it would not be fair to give the extremely intelligent people an advantage over others. However, we do not discover God through our minds, but through our spirits. "But a natural man does not accept the things of the Spirit of God, for they are foolishness to him; and *he cannot understand them, because they are spiritually appraised*" (1 Corinthians 2:14).

The Lord exists in the spiritual realm, so the way we communicate with Him is through our spirits. "God is spirit, and those who worship Him must worship in spirit and truth" (John 4:24). An astronaut cannot wear scuba equipment to do a space walk because space is in a completely different realm than the ocean. Scuba gear is fine for exploring underwater, but it is useless for exploring outer space. The spiritual realm is entirely different from the earthly realm, and they do not operate in the same way.

God wants a relationship with everyone—not just with intelligent people. It has been said that the Lord does not put His cookies on the top shelf where only a few can reach them, but on the bottom shelf where everyone can have them. Perhaps this is the reason Jesus said, "Truly I say to you, unless you are converted and become like children, you will not enter the kingdom of heaven" (Matthew 18:3). He made finding Him so simple that even a child can understand it.

When it comes to understanding spiritual truth, you must first turn off the button in your mind that only considers facts and figures to draw conclusions. While logic works fine for dealing with many earthly matters, it is the wrong means for accessing the spiritual realm. God cannot be found through human reasoning, but He will reveal Himself to those who will call out to Him with a sincere heart—like an infant cries for his or her mother.

4. God knows everything that will happen in the future

We have already examined a number of prophecies proving that God can accurately predict future events. Here are a few more verses where He claims to know the future:

> "Thus says the LORD, the King of Israel and his Redeemer, the LORD of hosts: 'I am the first and I am the last, and there is no God besides Me. Who is like Me? Let him proclaim and declare it; yes, let him recount it to Me in order, from the time that I established the ancient nation. And let them declare to them the things that are coming and the events that are going to take place. Do not tremble and do not be afraid; have I not long since announced it to you and declared it?'"
>
> Isaiah 44:6–8

> "Who has announced this from of old? Who has long since declared it? Is it not I, the LORD? And there is no other God besides Me, a righteous God and a Savior; there is none except Me."
>
> Isaiah 45:21

> "I am God, and there is no one like Me, declaring the end from the beginning, and from ancient times things which have not been done, saying, 'My purpose will be established, and I will accomplish all My good pleasure.'"
>
> Isaiah 46:9–10

Only God knows all the possible outcomes in any given situation—and even what *would have* happened in each case. He foresees the results of all your decisions, and He is able to lead you in the right way.

When Pharaoh let the people go, God did not lead them along the road to the land of the Philistines, even though it was nearby; for God said, "The people will change their minds and return to Egypt if they face war." So He led the people around toward the Red Sea along the road of the wilderness.

Exodus 13:17–18 HCSB

God knows everything that will occur in the future, which is called foreknowledge. Even though He knows exactly who, what and when everything will happen, that does not mean that He takes away your freedom to make your own decisions. He gives everyone a free will, which is why so much evil exists in the world. Some people choose to do horrific things. Even so, God is still in control and knows how every situation will turn out. God's foreknowledge is demonstrated in this passage:

And He sent two of His disciples and said to them, "Go into the city, and a man will meet you carrying a pitcher of water; follow him; and wherever he enters, say to the owner of the house, 'The Teacher says, "Where is My guest room in which I may eat the Passover with My disciples?"' And he himself will show you a large upper room furnished and ready; prepare for us there." The disciples went out and came to the city, and found it just as He had told them; and they prepared the Passover.

Mark 14:13–16

Notice five things that Jesus knew about the future:

- He knew when the two disciples entered the city that the appointed man would be at the right place to meet them, even though the man was unaware of the divine appointment.
- He knew the man would be carrying a pitcher of water, which was the sign for the disciples to identify him.
- He knew the man would lead His disciples to the right house.

- He knew the owner of the house would show them a large upper room.
- He knew the room would already be furnished.

Jesus could have personally escorted them to the upper room, but instead chose to send them ahead while accurately predicting what would happen to them in the city. Because Jesus chose this method, the amazing fulfillment of His prophecy would convince them that God was in control of the people and events in that situation.

Christ wanted His disciples to remember this incident because the circumstances were about to take an unexpected turn for the worse. In just a matter of hours, the miracle worker they had been following would be crucified beside criminals. It would appear to them that evil had won, which might make them think that the Lord was no longer in control.

To prepare them for this disturbing event—and to prove that God is in control even during the worst of times—Jesus foretold what was about to happen to Him. He explained that He would be betrayed, crucified, forsaken by the disciples and raised from the dead, and that Peter would deny that he even knew Him (see Mark 14:18, 24, 27, 28, 30). So when Jesus was arrested in the Garden of Gethsemane, the previously dedicated disciples scattered in fear because now their circumstances looked out of control.

Imagine how shocked these men must have been when the Roman soldiers nailed Jesus to a cross. Their fearless leader, who had done so many astonishing miracles, now appeared to be totally helpless. They could not understand why He was unable to do something as simple as stopping them from crucifying Him. It would be the perfect time to prove to everyone that He was in charge. It just did not make sense to them, even though Jesus had repeatedly told them that He would die and rise from the dead (see Matthew 16:21; 17:9, 22–23; 20:17–19; 26:2, 32, 45). He carefully explained to them that He must be killed so that "the Scriptures of the prophets might be fulfilled" (Matthew 26:56 NKJV).

Because God is all-powerful, He is able to take the evil deeds of men and use them for His purposes. The cross became the altar where Jesus would die for the sins of the world to purchase our salvation. Peter explained in his sermon on the day of Pentecost how God's big hand and the dirty little hands of men were at work at the same time.

> "This Man, delivered over by the *predetermined plan* and *foreknowledge of God*, you nailed to a cross by the hands of godless men and put Him to death."
>
> Acts 2:23

You are probably thinking, *If God knows the future, then that must mean everything that happens has already been determined and I cannot do anything about it.* But does the fact that God knows tomorrow mean that we have no choice? Of course not.

Suppose you record a football game on your DVR. The next day, you decide to watch the game. Did the players have a free will as they played the game? Yes they did, even though the outcome is already fixed on your recorder. More than likely the players who were more skilled, trained harder and made the fewest mistakes won the game.

If you fast-forward to the end, you can find out the final score. No matter how many times you watch it, the players still had a free will. And no matter how many times you view it, the final score will not change. But the final score did not determine how the game was played. Rather, how the game was played produced the final score.

God's foreknowledge is similar to watching earthly events on a DVR, except instead of watching after everything has been done, He sees beforehand what will happen. The fact that He knows the outcome does not negate the fact that everyone has a free will. He says, "Choose for yourselves today whom you will serve . . ." (Joshua 24:15).

You can choose to pick God's plan over your own. If you will place your little hand in God's big hand, He will lead you through this life. The apostle Paul says we are "working together with Him" (2 Corinthians 6:1).

The future has not happened yet, so the pages in the rest of the book of your life are still waiting to be written. You are writing the daily pages in your life's journal. God has a script for you to follow, which is the best plan for your life, but you can also follow your own way. You can choose how the book will read when your life is over, after the final page is written.

Now that you have caught a small glimpse of the vast, immeasurable knowledge of God, wouldn't it be foolish to try to live without Him? In Part Two, you will see that the Lord wants to personally speak to you and guide you through your life's journey.

➡ LEARNING TO TRUST

1. If trust comes from placing your confidence in another person, what are some things that we need to believe about God in order to place our trust in Him?

2. Jesus said that the Father knows when every sparrow falls to the ground and how much they are worth (see Matthew 10:29, 31). How does this information help to alleviate our fears?

3. Jesus said, "Indeed, the very hairs of your head are all numbered" (Luke 12:7). Why do you think He revealed this truth about God to us?

4. Why did Jesus shock His audience by talking about things that were humanly impossible? (See Mark 11:23–24.) How does this apply to the difficulties and problems that you face?

PART 2

DECIDING TO FOLLOW GOD

Face the facts. Uncertainty produces worry. Nothing worries you more than when you do not know what to do, or which way to turn. But if you could receive guidance from an all-knowing God, He could show you exactly what to do in every situation, which would alleviate much of your worrying.

It is not enough to say you trust the Lord. You must trust Him *with your life*. Worry is a matter of trust, but it is also a matter of control. You cannot trust God to control the circumstances in your life until you first ask Him to control your life. Although

83

He knows what is best for you, He cannot lead you in that plan until you first surrender to His control.

When a cowboy climbs on a horse that has not been ridden before, it will start bucking, trying to throw the rider off. But after a while, the horse submits to the rider and stops bucking. Only after the horse has been broken can it be guided wherever the rider wishes. To be guided by God, you must yield to His control, just as a horse submits to its rider.

The horse must learn how the cowboy communicates which way he wants to go. A gentle nudge on the sides and saying "giddyup" means to move forward. Pulling back on the reins and saying "whoa" means to stop. A slight tugging of the reins to either side signals to go right or left.

In the same way a horse is led, you must learn to be sensitive to how God leads you. How does He tell you to move forward? In what ways does He indicate you need to change course? How does He tell you what to do when you do not know what to do?

In this section, you will learn how to be led by God. How does this keep you from worrying? God always knows how to handle every situation that worries you. Once you learn how to follow God, He can show you where to go and what to do in any and every circumstance.

The Lord has a plan for your life and wants to guide you down the right path. These chapters will explain the various ways He will communicate with you as you seek to follow Him.

5

Placing Your Life in God's Hands

God reserves the very best for those who leave the choice with Him.

—Andrew Murray

When Jesus and His disciples arrive in Bethany, Martha welcomes them into her home. Immediately Martha hurries into the kitchen and starts preparing a meal for the crew. Meanwhile, her sister, Mary, heads to the other room where Jesus is teaching.

Martha is running around the kitchen gathering ingredients, and it really bothers her that Mary has not lifted a finger to help. God in the flesh is sitting in her home, revealing truths hidden from ages past, but Martha is too worried about getting the meal prepared to listen to a sermon. Mary sits at the feet of Jesus, taking in every word.

Finally, Martha stomps into the living room and interrupts the Bible study. With hands on her hips, she commands Jesus to do something about it. "Lord, do You not care that my sister has left me to do all the serving alone? Then tell her to help me" (Luke 10:40).

Jesus answers, "Martha, Martha, you are worried and bothered about so many things; but only one thing is necessary, for Mary has chosen the good part, which shall not be taken away from her" (Luke 10:41–42).

Martha was "worried and bothered." Does that describe you? Martha was worried and bothered about *so many* things because her priorities were out of whack. Jesus added, "But only one thing is necessary and Mary has chosen it."

I do not know what subject Jesus was teaching that day, but it would not surprise me if His sermon was "How to not be worried and bothered." Mary was listening. Martha was not.

These two sisters represent two very different ways to live. Most of us are like Martha—stressed out, trying to juggle our jam-packed schedules and checking items off our to-do lists. As a result, we are worried and bothered about so many things.

> The greatest hindrance keeping you from following Jesus is not Satan, but "Self."

But Jesus said Mary is to be our role model. She *chose* to seek guidance from Jesus. She took note of the things important to God. Mary knew if she would simply follow what He told her to do, she would experience the joyful and abundant life that He promised.

Jesus wants to teach you how to live so that you can enjoy life. He said, "Come to me, all of you who are weary and carry heavy burdens, and I will give you rest. Take my yoke upon you. *Let me teach you*, because I am humble and gentle at heart, and you will find *rest for your souls*" (Matthew 11:28–29 NLT). When you are constantly worried and bothered about life's pressures, your soul becomes exhausted, just as your body gets tired from running a marathon race.

Sleep gives you rest for your body, but only Jesus can provide rest for your soul. Worry is an invisible, heavy weight that you carry on your soul, which will drain your peace and joy. Would you like to experience a better way to live? You can, if you will place your life in God's hands.

A Better Way to Live

Jesus calls you to follow Him, but His invitation does not sound too warm and inviting. He said, "If anyone wishes to come after Me, he must deny himself, and take up his cross daily and follow Me" (Luke 9:23). Those words may not be what you want to hear, but they are actually the only remedy for a stressed-out life. Jesus said that three things are necessary to receive a better way of living.

1. Deny yourself

Jesus did not say that if you want to follow Him that you must deny Satan. The greatest hindrance keeping you from following Jesus is not Satan, but "Self." You must deny your Self, but what does that mean?

"Self" is actually *selfishness*. I know this might be hard for you to believe, but an extremely selfish person is living inside you. This self-centered individual is hiding inside you and is constantly trying to control you. When Jesus calls you to do something, the selfish person inside says, "No one is going to tell me what to do!"

Self only knows how to act selfishly. It lies to you, claiming to be your best friend when it is actually your worst enemy. It is only interested in being pampered. Self always demands its own way and is easily offended. It is the cause of every bad attitude and is the source of every marriage problem. Selfishness acts exactly opposite of Jesus.

Self is proud. Jesus is humble. "I am humble and gentle at heart" (Matthew 11:29 NLT).

Self wants to rule. Jesus came to serve. "The Son of Man did not come to be served, but to serve" (Matthew 20:28).

Self is rebellious. Jesus submitted to His Father. "I do not seek My own will, but the will of Him who sent Me" (John 5:30).

Now do you understand why Jesus said you must deny your Self? You cannot have both Self and God leading you at the same time.

2. *Take up your cross every day*

In the first century, criminals were executed on crosses. Once they died, they would never be able to cause trouble for anyone again. It would be nice if we could execute Self one time and it would be dead forever. Unfortunately, Self keeps resurrecting itself!

When you wake up in the morning, the selfish person inside gets up with you and starts bossing you around. It tells you what to think and how to act. Self needs to be crucified every day, which is why Jesus said, "take up your cross daily." So instead of waking up and listening to Self's orders, surrender your will to God before your feet hit the floor.

Admiral Horatio Nelson was an English navy hero who twice defeated Napoleon's army. Whenever he won in battle, he always treated his vanquished enemies with dignity. After one of his victories, a defeated opponent was brought on board Nelson's flagship for a formal ceremony of surrender. The custom called for the defeated admiral to surrender his sword, and then to shake hands.

The man marched across the quarterdeck wearing his saber and reached out to shake Nelson's hand. With his own hand remaining at his side, Nelson firmly decreed, "Your sword first—and then the hand."[1]

Surrendering means to quit fighting. Before you can be on God's side, you must first surrender your sword to Him. Come to God on His terms, not yours. Realize that He can guide your life better than you can.

3. Follow Him

What does it mean to follow Jesus? "Follow Me" does not mean to literally follow Him like the disciples did. No one living today can do that since Jesus is not physically here anymore. "Following Jesus" does not mean going somewhere with Him, but obeying what He tells you to do.

Jesus once cast demons out of a man. As He was getting into a boat to leave, the former demon-possessed man wanted to go with Him. Jesus told him, "Go home to your people and report to them what great things the Lord has done for you, and how He had mercy on you" (Mark 5:19). Although he did not physically follow Jesus, he *was* following Him because he obeyed what Christ told him to do.

God will reveal His plan to those who are willing to follow Him. Jesus said, "If anyone is *willing to do His will,* he will know of the teaching, whether it is of God" (John 7:17). You probably want to

> "Following Jesus" does not mean going somewhere with Him, but obeying what He tells you to do.

see where He wants to take you before making a commitment to Him. "Lord, first show me what your plan is, and if I like what I see, then I will consider doing it."

But God turns the order around. You must first commit to doing His will *before* He reveals His plan. He wants you to trust Him. First agree to do His will—and then you will know. If you are committed to obeying God's will, God is committed to revealing His will.

The Lord wants to show you the right path to follow in life, just like a shepherd leads his sheep to green pastures (see Psalm 23). The shepherd always knows what is best for the flock. Your role is to trust the Shepherd and follow wherever He leads. If you will do that, you will experience the most fulfilling, joyful life possible this side of heaven.

Discovering God's Plan for Your Life

It is not by accident that you are living on earth today and not in the 1300s. The Scripture says, "He made from one man every nation of mankind to live on all the face of the earth, *having determined their appointed times and the boundaries* of their habitation, that they would seek God, if perhaps they might grope for Him and find Him, though He is not far from each one of us" (Acts 17:26–27).

This verse says God determined *when* every nation would be in existence and *where* they would be located, which means He knew when and where you would be born. You are alive right now because the Lord has a purpose for you to fulfill during this earthly time period.

King David served the purpose of God in his own generation (see Acts 13:36). Just as David fulfilled God's purpose during his lifetime, the Lord wants you to complete your purpose in this generation. He put you on this planet for a reason—you have a destiny to fulfill.

The plan for your life begins when you join God's family. How can you call God your Father unless you are His child? When you receive Jesus Christ as your Lord, you are born spiritually and become a child of God. You came into this world by being physically born, but you enter the Kingdom of God by being born anew in your spirit.

Jesus came to earth to become the sacrifice for your sins. He lived a perfect life and when He died on the cross, He paid for the sins of the world, including yours. "He Himself bore our sins in His body on the cross, so that we might die to sin and live to righteousness" (1 Peter 2:24). Three days later, He rose from the dead and later ascended into heaven.

Although Jesus paid for your salvation, you must receive Him into your life to become a child of God. "But as many as received Him, to them He gave the right to become children of God, even to those who believe in His name" (John 1:12).

God wants everyone to be saved, so He extends this personal invitation to you. "This is good and acceptable in the sight of God our Savior, who desires all men to be saved and to come to the knowledge of the truth" (1 Timothy 2:3–4). You can be born spiritually by simply calling out to Him by faith. "Whoever will call upon the name of the Lord will be saved" (Romans 10:13). If you sincerely pray the following, He will save you:

> If you are committed to obeying God's will, God is committed to revealing His will.

Lord, I realize that I am a sinner and need Your forgiveness. Jesus, thank You for dying on the cross for my sins. Come into my life and save me. Wash me clean from every sin with Your blood. I give my life to You, and I will follow wherever You lead me. Amen.

If you sincerely said that prayer, your eternal destiny has just changed. You are now a child of God, your spiritual debts have been forgiven and heaven is your new eternal home. Welcome to the family of God!

Now the Lord has a script for you to follow during your remaining days on earth. God told Israel, "For I know the plans that I have for you . . . plans for welfare and not for calamity to give you a future and a hope" (Jeremiah 29:11). He not only had a plan for them, but He also has a plan for you, right now. The God who created and redeemed you also wants to guide you through this life so you can fulfill your destiny.

God does not reveal His plan like a blueprint that you see all at once, but as a scroll that is unrolled a little bit at a time. When you drive your car at night, your headlights will only shine so far. But as you keep driving, the headlights will move ahead with you and show you more. As you obey what He tells you to do, God will unveil His plan like the headlights in your car move ahead as you travel down life's road.

If God showed you everything about the rest of your life, you could not handle it. It would be overwhelming. Revealing a little bit at a time simplifies your life and keeps you from worrying. Jesus told His disciples, "I have many more things to say to you, but you cannot bear them now" (John 16:12). The disciples did not need to know some things until later, so there was no need for Jesus to tell them until the time was right. That is why you must trust God that He will reveal what you need to know *when* you need to know it.

The coming chapters will demonstrate the various ways God will communicate with you as He reveals His plan. All those things that "worry and bother" you will not annoy you anymore as you begin fulfilling your destiny.

➡ LEARNING TO TRUST

1. Martha was "worried and bothered about *so many* things," which indicates that she lived in a continual state of being stressed-out. What are some of the things that worry and bother you?

2. Jesus said only one thing is necessary and that Mary had chosen it. What do you think was that "one thing" that kept her from being worried and bothered?

3. Why did Jesus say that you must deny yourself before you can follow Him?

4. Jeremiah 29:11 says God had plans for Israel for welfare and not for calamity to give them a future and a hope. What does this say to people today who follow Him?

5. Read John 16:12. Why did Jesus tell His disciples that He would not reveal everything to them about the future? How can "living one day at a time" keep us from worrying?

6

Where Did That Thought Come From?

> Why is it that when we talk to God we're said to be praying, but when God talks to us we're schizophrenic?
>
> —Lily Tomlin

Some people believe that God does not speak to people today. They say we now have the Scriptures and that is all we need for guidance. Ironically, what they fail to realize that *it is from the Scriptures that we learn the Holy Spirit will speak directly to us and guide us* in our decisions. Jesus said:

> "I have many more things to say to you, but you cannot bear them now. But when He, the Spirit of truth, comes, He *will guide you* into all the truth; for He will not speak on His own initiative, but whatever He hears, *He will speak*; and *He will disclose to you* what is to come."
>
> John 16:12–13

God's written Word is the clearest revelation through which He will speak, so it is imperative that you spend time reading and studying it every day. Many of the answers you are looking for are found in the pages of the Bible.

Although God's Word gives wise counsel concerning how to live, it does not always give precise guidance for the variety of present-day circumstances you will face. One reason the Holy Spirit was sent is to speak to you and guide you in specific situations. Jesus said that the Holy Spirit "will disclose to you what is to come." In other words, the Spirit that indwells every believer will speak to your heart about how to proceed. You will know that it was the Lord speaking because it will always come to pass, or it will be confirmed in some other way.

When my minivan turned 100,000 miles, I thought it was a good time to sell it and buy another vehicle. After I prayed about the decision, I believed that the Lord was telling me to keep driving it until He showed me otherwise. For the next few years, our van continued to run virtually problem free except for normal maintenance. Nearly every day I prayed, *Lord, thank You that our van keeps running and hasn't had any problems.*

Eight years later, it had accumulated 190,000 miles. Every day as I drove to work, I thanked God for our van and that we had debt-free transportation. My wife, Cindy, also thanked God for our cars during her prayer time.

One Wednesday my wife was in our backyard watering some bushes when a thought popped into her mind. *Someone is going to give you a car.*

Those words caught Cindy completely off guard. *Someone is going to give us a car? Where did that thought come from?* she wondered. We had not been praying for another vehicle. However, if someone wanted to give us a car, we were not going to argue about it!

On Thursday evening a couple that we had recently met, Mike and Andrea, called to invite us over to their house for dinner on Friday. The following evening after we finished eating, Mike sat quietly, like he was thinking deeply about something. Finally he broke his silence.

"The real reason we invited you here was not just to eat a meal with us. We invited you here because God told us to give you our car. Andrea and I have a PT Cruiser that's only two years old, and we'd like for you to have it."

Andrea added, "Has the Lord given you any confirmation on this?"

Cindy's eyes got big as she remembered the words that came to her mind two days before. "I can confirm that. I was in my backyard on Wednesday when the Lord told me someone was going to give us a car."

During our 28 years of marriage, God had never told either one of us that someone would give us a car. But after the Lord spoke to Cindy, a car was given to us two days later!

God made His will unmistakably clear by speaking directly to Mike and Andrea, and to us. After we received the vehicle, we were able to extend the blessing by giving our van to someone who really needed it. And it all began with a thought that seemed to come out of nowhere.

Four Sources of Thoughts

One of the ways God speaks to us is through thoughts that He plants in our minds. Jesus once took His disciples to Caesarea Philippi, where Peter first confessed that Jesus was the Son of God. Now how did Peter know that fact? The Lord revealed that information to Peter by inserting a thought into his mind (see Matthew 16:13–17). Many times God speaks to us through that quiet voice in our minds.

Occasionally God speaks to people audibly, such as when Jesus was baptized (see Mark 1:11), when He was transfigured on the mountain (see Matthew 17:5) and when Saul heard Him speak in Hebrew on the road to Damascus (see Acts 26:14). However, talking in an audible voice is not His normal way of communicating with us today. The Lord typically speaks to us by placing ideas in our minds.

Maybe you just assumed that all those thoughts inside your mind originated with you, but you are not the only source for your ideas. Thoughts can originate from four different sources. You must use discernment to identify where the suggestions are coming from.

In a dialogue with His disciples at Caesarea, Jesus revealed the four sources of thoughts.

1. Some of our thoughts come from other people

Jesus asked His disciples, "Who do *people* say that the Son of Man is?" This question reveals one source for thoughts—the opinions of other people.

> Now when Jesus came into the district of Caesarea Philippi, He was asking His disciples, "Who do people say that the Son of Man is?" And they said, "Some say John the Baptist; and others, Elijah; but still others, Jeremiah, or one of the prophets."
>
> Matthew 16:13–14

We are greatly influenced by what other people think, which is not necessarily bad. That is how we learn—by digesting information from those who have done the research. We form our beliefs by embracing the ideas of others and making them our own.

The opinions of others can be a valid way to learn, but only if their information is correct. If the data is tainted or biased, you can be led astray. If a parent calls you "stupid," that wrong identity can get lodged inside your mind for years. When you embrace the false word, it becomes your own thought, even though it is inaccurate.

Your thoughts can originate from four different sources.

You can also be persuaded by propaganda. Special interest groups attempt to pressure you to think the way they do. The media wants you to think politically correct instead of spiritually correct. Some people do not want to think for themselves, so they conform to the opinions of the largest crowd, believing the majority must be right.

The way we think is shaped by information we receive from our parents, schoolteachers, friends, co-workers, the news media, television shows, books, the Internet and other people. With so many voices speaking to us, it is no wonder we are so confused. When everybody is saying something different, we do not know which source to believe. We are constantly bombarded with ideas that are simply not true.

The disciples had heard from others that Jesus was John the Baptist, Elijah, Jeremiah or one of the prophets that had risen from the dead. How did these rumors get started in the first place?

Someone came up with a theory of who He was and then passed it on to someone else who believed it, who told someone else and so on. Pretty soon, one group believed He was Elijah, while another bunch said He was Jeremiah. Still other groups thought He was one of the prophets that had risen from the dead. Obviously, they could not all be right. In fact, they were all wrong.

Herod believed that Jesus was John the Baptist back from the dead. He said, "John, whom I beheaded, has risen!" (Mark 6:16). He actually believed that John had been resurrected and put his head back on—which, of course, was not true. Ironically, when Jesus rose from the dead on the third day, which *was* true, Herod dismissed it as a rumor. Both reports were accounts of miraculous resurrections, but the king chose to believe the lie instead of the truth.

We are faced with the same proposition today. Which voices will we listen to and believe? The ideas we receive from others are a mixture of truth and error, and it is our responsibility to sort fact from fiction.

2. Most of our thoughts come from ourselves

After questioning His disciples about what others thought of Him, Jesus then asked what *they* thought. "But who do *you* say that I am?" (Matthew 16:15). It goes without saying that we have a mind of our own. We can think up our own thoughts from within.

The National Science Foundation says that the average person has about twelve thousand thoughts per day. A deep thinker can have fifty thousand daily thoughts.[1] How they figured this out, I will never know. Did some guy in a white lab coat hold a counter in his hand and click it each time a thought popped into his head?

With so many thoughts scurrying through our craniums, it is a miracle in itself that any two people can think alike about anything. "Can't we all just get along?" Even when people are tracking the same, we are still not going to agree on every point. The apostle Paul said, "One person regards one day above another, another regards every day alike. Each person must be fully convinced *in his own mind*" (Romans 14:5).

We all have our "own mind," and the way we think may be right or wrong. For this reason, you must "be transformed by the renewing of your mind, so that you may prove what the will of God is, that which is good and acceptable and perfect" (Romans 12:2).

3. God can also plant thoughts in our minds

The Lord is a third source for our thoughts. When Nehemiah was directed by God to go to Jerusalem and rebuild the wall, he said, "I did not tell anyone what my *God was putting into my mind* to do for Jerusalem" (Nehemiah 2:12). The entire plan began with the Lord putting thoughts into his mind. After the wall was built, Nehemiah said, "*God put it into my heart* to assemble the nobles" (Nehemiah 7:5). Again we see that the Lord was communicating what He wanted done by speaking to Nehemiah's inner being.

I once asked God, "Lord, this universe is so huge and I'm so little. Why would You want to speak to me?" Immediately the thought came to my mind, *I don't want to talk only to you. I want to talk to everybody else in the world, too.*

I had never thought about that before. God does want to speak to everyone, but many people do not want anything to do with Him. If you want to hear from the Lord, you must open your heart and be willing to obey His voice.

A woman I know named Judie was praying for her friend Karla, who was going through some trials. The Lord spoke to Judie, *Go tell Karla, "Everything is going to be okay, My little cheese."*

Judie thought, *My little cheese? What does that mean?*

Even though it made no sense to her, she delivered the word to Karla. Immediately Karla started crying. She said, "When I was a little girl, 'little cheese' is what family members called me as a term of endearment, to assure me that everything would be okay." Although Judie did not know this fact about Karla, the Lord did, and it was exactly what she needed to hear.

God always speaks what is true because He is the Spirit of Truth and it is impossible for Him to lie (see Hebrews 6:18). He speaks primarily through His written Word, the Bible, which is the clearest revelation of His will, but He will also speak to our minds. When God puts a thought in someone's mind, it will never contradict the teachings of the Bible. We see an example of how God can speak to a person's mind when Peter answered Jesus' question.

> Peter answered, "You are the Christ, the Son of the living God." And Jesus said to him, "Blessed are you, Simon Barjona, because flesh and blood did not reveal this to you, but My Father who is in heaven."
>
> Matthew 16:16–17

Sometimes it is hard to distinguish between our thoughts and God's. Both thoughts seem the same to us. Here we see that God dropped a thought into Peter's mind, although he did not seem to be aware of this fact. Peter told Jesus that He was the Christ, the Son of God. Jesus had to reveal to Peter that the Father had planted that thought in his mind. Otherwise, Peter would have believed that he came up with that idea on his own.

Jesus said, "Peter, you didn't come up with that thought. My Father planted that idea in your mind."

Apparently, that thought from God seemed just like Peter's own thoughts. This conversation gives us an interesting insight into God's guidance. Many times when the Lord speaks to us, we assume those thoughts are our own. In other words, sometimes we are not aware that God is speaking to us.

Jesus had to reveal to Peter that the Father had planted that thought in his mind.

God's words will usually come into your mind disguised as your own thoughts. Have you ever had an unusual thought pop into your mind completely out of the blue? An idea that you did not think up on your own? This was how God told Pete Shultis to marry the choir girl (see chapter 1), and how He spoke to my wife about the car. Sometimes God will give a revelation about something you could not have known without Him telling you.

Peter Lord, the author of the bestselling book *Hearing God,* was the pastor of Park Avenue Baptist Church in Titusville, Florida, for many years. A number of years ago in December, Peter was praying when a thought came to his mind:

I want you to construct a building where people can pray. As proof that this is My idea and not yours, I will send someone to the church that you don't know who will give five hundred dollars toward the building. Peter wrote down in his prayer journal what the Lord had said.

> Many times when the Lord speaks to us, we assume those thoughts are our own.

The next day as he was praying about the chapel, another thought came to him: *This will happen before Christmas.* Again, Peter wrote down what God had told him, but he did not tell anyone.

A week passed. No one brought him any money. Two weeks went by, but still no answer, so he started to doubt. He prayed, "Lord, are You sure You didn't mean by New Year's Day?" He did not hear a response from God.

Then a few days before Christmas, a married couple from another city pulled into the church parking lot. They walked into church and introduced themselves to Peter.

"Pastor, you don't know us, but when we were praying God spoke to us. He told us to come here and give you some money. We don't really understand why we needed to drive here to give this to you, but we're just being obedient." The couple then handed him a check for five hundred dollars![2]

God fulfilled what He had spoken both to Peter and to the couple who had driven from out of town. The Lord orchestrated this divine appointment, where an unknown couple donated the exact amount God had revealed to Peter, which was confirmation that the prayer chapel needed to be built.

4. Satan can interject thoughts into our minds to deceive us

We should not assume that every thought that enters our minds comes from God, or even ourselves. The devil is the fourth source of thoughts.

After Jesus told Peter that the Father had spoken to him, Peter probably figured that the Lord had appointed him to deliver other messages to God's Son. Not much later, another email arrived in the inbox of Peter's mind, this time with a virus attached. Playing the role of prophet, Peter told Jesus, "God told me to tell You not to go to the cross."

> From that time Jesus began to show His disciples that He must go to Jerusalem, and suffer many things from the elders and chief priests and scribes, and be killed, and be raised up on the third day. Peter took Him aside and began to rebuke Him, saying, "God forbid it, Lord! This shall never happen to You."
>
> Matthew 16:21–22

Peter thought he was delivering another message from God, but Jesus revealed that this time his suggestion was coming from the devil. Apparently both thoughts, one from the Father and the other from Satan, sounded exactly the same to him.

> But He turned and said to Peter, "Get behind Me, Satan! You are a stumbling block to Me; for you are not setting your mind on God's interests, but man's."
>
> Matthew 16:23

After God put a thought in Peter's mind, Satan also planted an idea. This shows how quickly the sources of our thoughts can change and why we need to use discernment.

Why did Satan plant a thought in Peter's mind after God had put a thought in his mind? He wanted to use one of Jesus' closest followers as a mouthpiece to deceive Him. The devil wanted Jesus to believe that this suggestion was also coming from His Father. Jesus identified and rebuked the sinister source of the message.

Satan is your spiritual enemy, and he has the ability to plant thoughts in your mind to deceive you. Jesus revealed the true nature of Satan. "There is no truth in him. Whenever he speaks a lie, he speaks from his own nature; for he is a liar and the father of lies" (John 8:44). His goal is to make your life as miserable as possible by injecting thoughts of fear, anger, depression, jealousy and worry.

You should never believe every thought that pops into your mind. You must identify where the thought is coming from before acting on it.

There is a humorous story about a man who comes home from work. When he walks into his house, he hears a voice say, "Quit your job, sell your house, take your money, go to Vegas." The man is disturbed by what he hears, so he ignores the voice.

The next day after he gets home, the same thing happens. The voice tells him, "Quit your job, sell your house, take your money, go to Vegas."

Again the man ignores the voice, although he is very troubled to hear it again.

Every day for a week, the man hears the same voice when he gets home from work, giving the same instructions. Finally, he gives in. He quits his job, sells his house, takes his money and heads to Vegas.

The moment he gets off the plane in Vegas, the voice says, "Go to Harrah's Casino." Immediately he hops in a cab and hurries over to Harrah's.

As soon as he sets foot in the casino, the voice speaks again. "Go to the roulette table." The man does as he is told.

When he gets to the roulette table, the voice says, "Put all your money on 17."

Nervously, the man cashes in his money for chips and puts them all on 17. The dealer wishes the man good luck and spins the roulette wheel. The ball goes around and around. The man anxiously watches the ball as it slowly loses speed until finally it settles into . . . number 21.

The voice says, "Crud!"

Remember, not every voice in your mind is God speaking to you. Examine where each thought is coming from. Is it telling you to trust the Lord? Or is it tormenting you with worry?

➡ LEARNING TO TRUST

1. Even though God's written Word is the clearest revelation of His will, why is it also important for us to be led by the Holy Spirit?

2. How can you usually know when God has put a thought in your mind and that it is not your own idea?

3. If thoughts come into your mind that contradict the principles in God's Word, what can you conclude about them?

4. Why do think that Peter could not distinguish between the thought from God and the message from Satan? What can we learn from this about being discerning?

7

Guidance Through Dreams

Put your dream to the test. If it is from God, it should pass the criteria for true guidance.

—Bob Mumford

Carolyn Eckman, a missionary to Irian Jaya, Indonesia, awakened one night from a terrifying dream with her heart beating wildly. In her dream, she was driving along the tortuous two-lane road that led to the coastal city of Jayapura. She had her family with her, and they were on their way to the market.

She came to a section of road that was being repaired. Only one lane of traffic was open and it led around a tight, blind curve. A spray of yellow-green bamboo overhung the road on the left side.

Just as she came to the curve, in her dream, a blue Volkswagen minibus with yellow taxicab license plates came hurtling around the curve. The two vehicles crashed head-on, scattering car parts and human body parts all over the road. The horrifying vividness of the dream made returning to sleep very difficult.

The next afternoon Carolyn was in her car on the way to Jayapura for the once-a-week duty of helping the new missionaries learn the Indonesian language. She came to a blind curve where repairs had reduced the road to a single lane. She noticed the bright yellow-green bamboo shoots on her left. It was the same curve she had seen in her dream the night before!

She did exactly what you or I would have done; she pulled off to the side of the road as far as she could get. Suddenly, screeching around that blind corner, came a blue Volkswagen minibus with yellow taxicab license plates. It would have certainly hit her if she had not pulled off the road as she did. God had spared her life by warning her in a dream![1]

In the same way God plants thoughts in our minds while we are awake, He can also project images in our minds while we are asleep. Many times in Scripture the Lord spoke to people through their dreams. God gave dreams to Abimelech, Jacob, Laban, Joseph, Pharaoh, Gideon's enemy, Solomon, King Nebuchadnezzar, Joseph the husband of Mary, and Paul. Since God communicated information in this way to people in the Bible, we must consider dreams as a valid way He can speak to us.

Let me make one thing clear. While the Lord may occasionally speak to us through a dream, most dreams are not messages sent from God. Even so, the apostle Peter confirmed the Old Testament prophet Joel's prediction that in the last days "your young men shall see visions, and your old men shall dream dreams" (Acts 2:17; see Joel 2:28). The last days began on the day of Pentecost and will extend until the end of the age, so that means He is still communicating to His people in this way.

The Lord speaks to us through dreams to guide us in a visual way so that we will know what to do, or to warn us about danger so we can avoid it (see Matthew 2:12, 22). He communicates in this way to those who are submitted to doing what He wants. By using various forms of communication, He can reveal things to us both while we are awake and also when we are sleeping.

Satan can also put thoughts in our minds while we are sleeping. He can give dreams and nightmares to disturb us, to lead us down the wrong path, or to cause confusion. If your dream leads you away from the Lord and His ways, you will know that it did not come from God. If you are continually tormented by nightmares, you must submit yourself to the Lord and rebuke them using the name of Jesus.

I once prayed for a man who had the same recurring nightmare every night for eight years. Jeremy was a professional bodyguard, and he had fought and killed a man who tried to attack the client he was protecting. Every night after the incident, Jeremy had the same agonizing dream of hand-to-hand combat with the man. He put holes in the walls as he acted out what he was dreaming. This went on *every night* for eight years, until he asked for prayer.

As we rebuked the nightmare in Jesus' name, he started getting an excruciating headache. He then felt something leave him, and his headache immediately stopped. At that point, he became extremely sleepy and went home to go to bed. His horrible dream has never come back after that!

How do you know if a dream is from God? It will typically seem different from other dreams, and usually feels more real or vivid. Dreams from God will be in harmony with the Scriptures and the interpretation will give you better insight into a specific situation. If you do not know the interpretation, you should pray and ask the Lord to reveal it to you. Sometimes He will give the interpretation to someone else, as in some of the cases listed below.

Purposes for Dreams

Why would God give you a dream without also having a purpose for it? Whenever the Lord speaks through a dream, He will also reveal its meaning. In the Old Testament, a couple of prisoners had dreams and wanted to know the interpretations. Their fellow prisoner Joseph said, "Do not interpretations [of dreams] belong to God?" (Genesis 40:8). He then explained the meaning of their dreams so they could know what was going to happen to them. Here are several reasons why God speaks to people through dreams.

1. Dreams can confirm God's will

When Mary became pregnant through a miracle of the Holy Spirit, her fiancé, Joseph, was understandably confused and heartbroken because they had not had sexual relations. No woman in the history of the world had ever become pregnant without knowing a man, so he had good reason to believe she had been unfaithful. He decided to secretly divorce her.

To keep him from making a huge mistake, the Lord interrupted his plans by speaking to him in an unusual way. An angel appeared to him in a dream and said, "Do not be afraid to take Mary as your wife; for the Child who has been conceived in her is of the Holy Spirit" (Matthew 1:19–20). As a result of this revelation, Joseph took her as his wife and protected her virginity until she gave birth.

This would not be the last time God would speak to him through a dream. After Mary gave birth to Jesus, King Herod became jealous that a rival king had been born in Israel. In an effort to eliminate the competition, he gave orders to kill all the male children in Bethlehem two years old and younger.

Knowing what Herod had planned to do, the Lord warned Joseph in a dream to take Mary and baby Jesus to Egypt and remain there until Herod died. This revelation through a dream sent them to a specific place, which was also a fulfillment of a prophecy given by Hosea over seven hundred years before: "Out of Egypt I called My son" (Hosea 11:1; Matthew 2:15).

After Herod died, the Lord spoke to him through a third dream and instructed them to go back to Israel. In Joseph's dreams, the Lord revealed exactly when to leave and where to go and when and where to return. Although God could have chosen another way to speak to him, the dreams were evidently the best way to communicate this information.

When the apostle Paul was on his second missionary journey, he had a dream about a man calling out to him, "Come over to Macedonia and help us." As a result of the vision in the night, he decided to travel to Macedonia "concluding that God had called us to preach the gospel to them" (Acts 16:9–10). Paul understood that the Lord had chosen to speak to him in a night vision, and his conclusion proved to be correct. This shows one of the reasons God gives dreams—to confirm His will to us.

In another case, God reduced Gideon's army to just three hundred men. To give Gideon assurance that he would be victorious against the Midianites, the Lord told him to go to the enemy's camp and he would hear something that would encourage him. When he got to the camp, he heard two Midianite soldiers talking.

> When Gideon came, behold, a man was relating a dream to his friend. And he said, "Behold, I had a dream; a loaf of barley bread was tumbling into the camp of Midian, and it came to the tent and struck it so that it fell, and turned it upside down so that the tent lay flat." His friend replied, "This is nothing less than the sword of Gideon the son of Joash, a man of Israel; God has given Midian and all the camp into his hand."
>
> When Gideon heard the account of the dream and its interpretation, he bowed in worship.
>
> Judges 7:13–15

God gave his enemy the dream and then led Gideon to the Midianite camp at just the right time so he could overhear the conversation. Then the Lord gave the interpretation of the dream to the other man so that it would confirm God's will to Gideon.

When my wife and I planted a church in Kansas, we searched for years to find some property that our congregation could afford. During that time, the cost of land kept escalating. Whenever we found a piece of property at a reasonable price, the door always slammed shut.

When we first began our search, we thought four acres would be enough land. But as the church continued to grow, it became apparent that we needed at least ten acres. Most properties were selling for $45,000 per acre, and we did not have the money to purchase ten acres at that price.

After years of looking, I was getting desperate. I wondered why God had not provided land for His church after many years of praying. I pleaded with Him one more time. *Lord, Walmart had no problem getting land for their building. Where is the land for Your church? We want souls to be saved and that's more important than a retail store. I know You must have some land for us. Please show us where it is.*

While I was praying about this, a thought that came out of nowhere said, *Eighth Street.* It took me by surprise because I had looked everywhere else in town, but never on Eighth Street. At first I dismissed it, assuming that the thought must have come from myself.

Over the next few days, I continued to ask God for land. And every time I prayed, *Eighth Street* came to my mind. I have learned that when God speaks, He usually reinforces His will by repeating the thoughts until I finally get the message. I went to a Realtor in our church and asked him to find out if any property was for sale on Eighth Street.

Meanwhile, I drove to Eighth Street, which was mostly undeveloped farmland. I found a vacant lot at the north end of the road on the east side, which was next to a main highway. It looked like the perfect place for a church. *This must be the land that God wants us to have,* I thought.

A few days later a church member came to me and said, "Pastor, I had a dream last night. I saw our new church building had been built on Eighth Street."

I was shocked to hear him say "Eighth Street" because no one in the church other than the Realtor knew we were looking there. I was curious if he had seen the same property in the dream that I had wanted. "Was the property at the north end of the street on the east side next to the highway?"

"No, it wasn't. The land was on the south end of Eighth Street on the west side."

The Lord had confirmed Eighth Street but I did not know exactly where on that road.

Not long after this, the Realtor returned with his report. "I found property on Eighth Street that just became available this week. People have been trying to buy this land for years but it hasn't been for sale until now. Two land developers also want it, but the owners said they will let us have the first option to buy it at a reduced price."

"Is the land at the north end on the east side, next to the highway?" I asked.

He said, "No, it's on the south end on the west side of the street."

> God usually reinforces His will by repeating the thoughts until we finally get the message.

The property for sale was the exact location that the man had seen in his dream! He had no way of knowing we were looking on Eighth Street or that this property had just become available. God made the right location abundantly clear through three confirmations: His voice saying "Eighth Street," the property going up for sale that week and the man's dream pinpointing the exact spot.

During the years we were looking for land, this property was not for sale. But the moment it went on the market, the Lord immediately told us where it was. We purchased 22 acres of land for an incredibly low price of just $55,000. Because we bought the property at a bargain price, we were able to construct our church facility debt-free.

Here are some important facts concerning how the Lord brought it all together.

- We were willing to wait for God to provide in His timing. During the waiting time, our church saved enough money to purchase the land and construct our building debt-free.
- God planted the thought "Eighth Street" in my mind to show me the general location of the property.
- At the same time I received the idea from God, the land was put up for sale.
- The Realtor did his homework and found the property for sale.
- The Lord confirmed the exact location through a dream of a church member who did not know we were searching for property on that street.

We would have never purchased the property simply on the basis of a church member's dream, but God gave him the remarkable dream as confirmation to our board that we were making the correct decision.

2. Dreams can give you insight into situations

God told King Solomon that he could ask for whatever he wanted. Solomon asked for wisdom and became the wisest person on the planet. Most people overlook the fact that the Lord spoke to him in a dream. After receiving the revelation where God promised him wisdom, riches, honor and long life, "then Solomon awoke, and behold, it was a dream" (1 Kings 3:15).

Suppose Solomon had woken up thinking, *Wow, what a crazy dream. Imagine, God wants to make me the wisest person on the planet. Um, I don't think so!*

He could have easily dismissed it as just another dream. Instead, he recognized it for what it was—a revelation from the Most High God that would change his life forever. He embraced the promise and received insight into solving problems. God can use dreams to impart wisdom to us as well.

Steve was a new Christian who had a tarnished past. Because he did not understand the Bible, he wanted to find someone who would teach him the ways of God. Alan, who was a friend from church, agreed to take him under his wing and mentor him. Alan had never mentored anyone before and did not know how to do it. Whenever they got together, Alan would tell him what he should and should not do, but Steve kept struggling and slipping back into his old ways.

One night, Alan dreamed that he was on a two-lane highway when he encountered an elephant standing in the road. He tried pushing the elephant from behind, but it would not budge. Then he walked around to the front and tried pulling on its trunk, but it still would not move. Frustrated with the stubborn elephant, Alan gave up trying to move the animal. As he continued walking down the road, the elephant started walking with him. Immediately Alan woke up and knew the interpretation.

In their next mentoring meeting, Alan said, "Steve, I've tried pushing you and pulling you, but nothing has worked. I've decided that I'm just going to walk down the road of life. If you want to join me, I'll teach you everything that I've learned as we walk together."

Alan's dream gave him an insight concerning how to mentor those who want to be disciples. Mentoring is not just giving wise advice, but walking down the road together and teaching along the way. Alan said his informal mentoring technique worked wonderfully.

A number of years ago I had a vivid dream that was a revelation from God. Whenever the Holy Spirit gives a dream, it will always be consistent with the Scriptures, and its message will have a clear interpretation.

In my dream, I was in a huge medieval castle like one you would see in the movies. As I was walking down the stairs, gigantic gray pit bulls with glowing red eyes came out of hidden doors and attacked me one after another. I successfully fought off the vicious dogs with my sword. But every time I turned a corner, another beast would come out and try to pounce on me. Although none of them hurt me, I was getting exhausted from fighting so many pit bulls.

Finally I got to the bottom of the stairs and entered an enormous room. A witch was sitting on a couch in the middle of the room, laughing at me as if I were completely helpless. I could not figure out why she seemed so confident, like she had power over me. I had just defeated every pit bull that had attacked me, but she appeared to have more authority than all the other beasts I had faced.

Suddenly I realized the secret of defeating her. I looked straight into the witch's eyes and said, "I forgot one thing. *Holiness!*"

As soon as I said *holiness*, she let out a bloodcurdling shriek, "Nooooooo . . . !" and fled out of the room. Immediately the dream ended and I woke up.

I instantly knew the interpretation. The pit bulls that were attacking me represented demons, and the witch that laughed at me was Satan. The sword I had used to defeat the demons was God's Word (see Ephesians 6:17). The witch shrieked in horror because I had discovered that holiness is the key to spiritual victory. The Holy Spirit is the Spirit of holiness. Walking in the Spirit not only gives us tremendous power to defeat the enemy, but it also keeps the doors closed through which demons attack.

I believe God gave me that dream and interpretation to share with Christians who constantly struggle with temptation. They have forgotten about the importance of walking in holiness. Satan is constantly attacking them, and they are exhausted from fighting one battle after another. Although they know God's Word, they have compromised their integrity. The secret to winning spiritual battles is not trying to fight off evil and temptation. Victory comes by yielding to the Holy Spirit so He can completely control your life. "Walk by the Spirit, and you will not carry out the desire of the flesh" (Galatians 5:16).

Satan laughs when you try to fight spiritual battles using the power of the flesh, which is your own human strength. That strategy is guaranteed to fail. Giving in to temptations opens doors for demonic attacks—battles you should not be fighting. However, if you will walk in the Spirit, it keeps many of the pit bulls behind the doors, cuts off their opportunities to attack and reduces your temptations. Holiness is produced when you allow the Holy Spirit to empower you to live a life that is pleasing to God. Walking in holiness reduces the number of spiritual battles you fight and actually makes your life peaceful.

The Holy Spirit's first name is *Holy*. His name is not the Power Spirit, although He does give us power. Power without holiness is nothing more than witchcraft. He is also not called the Joyful Spirit, although He does give us joy. His power works through His holiness, and He fills us with joy when we walk in the Spirit.

God sometimes gives dreams to unbelievers because the information will benefit others. The Lord gave a dream to a pagan Egyptian Pharaoh so that Joseph and Israel would be blessed. He spoke to King Abimelech in a dream to protect Sarah, and to Laban on behalf of Jacob.

The Lord is the source of all true knowledge and can bestow it on whomever He wishes—even those who are atheists. He will give insights for the betterment of mankind because "He causes His sun to rise on the evil and the good, and sends rain on the righteous and the unrighteous" (Matthew 5:45).

Elias Howe invented the lockstitch sewing machine in 1845. I cannot tell you if Howe had a relationship with the Lord, but he received the idea for his invention in a dream. He wrote that he got the breakthrough concept of moving the needle with the hole to the "wrong end" while sleeping.

In his dream, Howe was in the jungles of Africa and had been captured by cannibals. As they prepared to cook him in a huge pot of water, they were dancing around the fire waving their spears. Howe noticed the up-and-down motion of the spears, and how the head of each spear had a small hole through the shaft.

After he awoke, he thought, *Holes in the points . . . holes in the points. That's the answer!*

He applied the concept from his dream to his sewing machine. The idea of passing the thread through the needle close to the point, and not at the other end, was a major innovation in making mechanical sewing possible. His dream led to the realization of the Industrial Revolution.[2]

3. Dreams can reveal the future

In the Old Testament, God gave Joseph two dreams. When he was seventeen years old, Joseph dreamed he was gathering sheaves with his brothers. His bundle of wheat stood erect as his brothers' sheaves bowed down to him. His brothers correctly interpreted the dream—that Joseph would rule over them. It was followed by another dream where the sun, moon and eleven stars bowed down to him, which meant that his father, mother and eleven brothers would submit to him (see Genesis 37:5–10). Twenty-two years later, his two dreams came to pass.

When Joseph was in an Egyptian prison, the Pharaoh had two dreams about the future. In the first, he saw seven fat cows and seven skinny cows by the Nile River. The seven skinny cows swallowed up the fat cows. It puzzled Pharaoh so much that he woke up.

He went back to sleep and dreamed he saw seven plump ears of grain on a single stalk. Then seven thin ears of grain swallowed up the seven plump ears. Again, Pharaoh woke up as soon as the dream ended.

Joseph interpreted both dreams and said, "Pharaoh's dreams are one and the same; *God has told to Pharaoh what He is about to do*" (Genesis 41:25). He explained that seven years of bumper crops would be followed by seven years of famine. He instructed Pharaoh to store up grain during the seven bountiful years to prepare for the seven years of famine. Pharaoh was so impressed with Joseph's ability to interpret the dreams that he promoted him to the second highest position in Egypt.

From these strange dreams, we learn that no matter how bizarre they may be, it could be God speaking! All four of the dreams pertained to the future, and the Lord revealed two of them to a man who would be considered a pagan.

Sometimes the Lord will give a dream about something that will happen in the future so the recipient will respond to the information. Jim Green, executive director of The *Jesus* Film Project, wrote in his monthly report:

A *Jesus* film team was driving to a film showing site in a Muslim nation. . . . They prayed that God would go before them and open doors of opportunity and give them safety. Just before they arrived at the village, a policeman flagged down their car. It seemed that an Islamic teacher needed a ride. The officer made the introductions and asked if they could help. Feeling it was an acceptable and necessary risk, they agreed and offered a ride, and continued towards town.

You can imagine the anxiety the team must have felt when this highly respected teacher asked, "Tell me, are you the ones planning to tell people about God?" Entrusting themselves to the Lord, they responded, "Yes, we are." Apprehension turned to astonishment as . . . the teacher told the team how he had experienced a unique dream. "I was told [in the dream] to come to this spot in the road, at this time, and that I would encounter someone who would tell me about God. It must be you."[3]

The team gave him some literature and invited him to see the film that night, which he did. It was no accident that the team arrived at the exact spot in the road that the Muslim man had seen in his dream.

God can give dreams about a future event so that we can be prepared for it. Several years ago I dreamed about a cruel man who was a member of the church where I had been pastor. This highly critical man was one of the main reasons I had left that church. He and his wife were "pastor abusers"—harsh church members who verbally attack their ministers to make their lives miserable.

In my dream I saw him falsely accusing me, just as he had done while I was his pastor. When the dream ended, I immediately woke up and it was morning. I began praying for my enemy, asking the Lord to change his heart. I had not seen the man since I had left the church, which was ten months earlier.

That day I went to the mall, which was about fifteen miles away from my home. While I was standing in front of a store, the cruel man almost bumped right into me. Apparently he had not seen me until the last moment. What are the odds that our paths would cross just hours after I had seen him in the dream?

Instead of feeling intimidated by him, I was overwhelmed with God's peace and I even felt compassion for him. When I greeted him, he quickly turned away from me. I thought, *Lord, thank You for speaking to me. You gave me that dream four hours ago because You knew I would see him today.*

That was many years ago and the only time that I have seen the antagonistic man was on the day I dreamed about him. The Lord gave me that dream so I would pray for my enemy and to prepare my heart for the encounter.

Again, let me reinforce that most of your dreams are not messages from God. But when He does speak to you in this unique way, make sure you obey what He is asking you to do.

Years ago, my brother-in-law worked in a glass factory. One night he dreamed that a certain area would have an accident where a large amount of glass would shatter. He figured it must be God warning him, so he roped off the area so that no one would get hurt in case it happened. Three days later the glass collapsed in that exact spot!

Although God has many other ways to speak to us, do not dismiss your dreams so quickly. If you do, you just might miss a message from God.

➤ LEARNING TO TRUST

1. What are some reasons that God gives dreams?

2. How can a dream from God guide you in making a correct decision? (See Matthew 1:19–20; Acts 16:9–10.)

3. Why is it important to embrace a dream from God and not dismiss it? (See 1 Kings 3:5–15.)

4. How can a dream from God help you not to worry about the future?

8

God Speaks Through Others

Never confuse the will of the majority with the will
of God.

—Chuck Colson

When I was in college, I often wondered how I would find my
future wife. I had quit dating girls who did not have a relationship
with God. One of my friends poked fun at me for not putting
forth more effort in trying to find her. He mocked, "Crockett,
do you think your wife is just going to call you on the phone
and say, 'Here I am'?"

I knew that only God knew where she was and only He could
to bring us together, so I put my complete trust in Him to make
it happen. As it turned out, my wife lived three hundred miles
from where I went to college. Even if God had revealed to me the
city where she lived, how would I find her if I traveled there? If
God had told her that I was a college student on a large campus,
how would she have found me?

Obviously, we could not find each other on our own. So how did we find each other? God arranged a divine appointment. Here is how it happened.

After my friend Blaine returned from working on summer staff at Glorieta Baptist Conference Center in New Mexico, I gave him a call to ask how his summer had gone. After we talked awhile, Blaine commented, "Kent, next summer you need to go work on staff at Glorieta."

I had never been to that place and had no interest in going there, so I just continued our conversation without commenting on it. I did not realize that God had spoken through my friend and his suggestion would change my destiny!

When I returned to college that fall, the words Blaine had spoken kept coming to my mind, *"Kent, next summer you need to go work on staff at Glorieta."* I could not get his words out of my head.

Why do I keep thinking about working on staff at a Baptist conference center in New Mexico? I wondered. *I am not even a Baptist. It must be 900 miles from home. Why would I want to go there?*

I finally decided to call the place and ask for an application. The person who answered the phone said, "I'll be glad to send you a form. However, you must realize that we receive about three thousand applications for our summer staff positions and we can only choose three hundred."

Since only 10 percent of the applicants were hired, I assumed they would not choose me, being a non-Baptist. Still, I figured I had nothing to lose by sending in my application. To my surprise, a few weeks later I received a letter saying that I had been accepted to work on their staff.

At the end of the school year, I traveled 866 miles across Texas to the mountains of New Mexico. I was pleased to find out that the Baptist camp was not a monastery as I had envisioned it. Half of the staff workers were college-age females.

A few weeks into the summer, I noticed a cute girl walking across the campus eating a candy bar. She tossed the wrapper on the ground, and her littering gave me an excuse to talk to her.

"Hey, don't you know it's against the law to litter on Baptist property?" I announced like the candy bar cop, with a big smile on my face. I reached down and picked up the wrapper. "I'll let it go this time," I flirted, "but don't let it happen again."

"Yes, sir," she replied, flirting back. "I'll make sure if I ever do it again that you're not around." I could tell she liked me. It was the beginning of a wonderful summer.

She swept me off my feet and we were married two and a half years later. Cindy has been my best friend, the mother of our two wonderful children and a counselor to many women through her ministry as a pastor's wife. And, thanks to my admonition, she has never littered since then.

Neither of us could have planned this divine appointment. We lived hundreds of miles apart, but God led us both to same place so our paths would cross.

As I reflect on our lives and connect the dots, the first dot that started our journey together came from what seemed to be a casual remark through a friend of mine a year before I met Cindy. God spoke through my friend to put a thought in my mind. If he had not made that suggestion, I would have never gone there because it was of no interest to me.

This experience was just one of the many times God has spoken to me through other people. Sometimes the messages have concerned small matters, while at other times they have been life-changing. In some cases, God has spoken through someone in a casual conversation where the words jumped out at me like a flashing neon light.

> If you want the Lord to continue speaking to you, you must obey what He has already revealed to you.

A woman once told me, "My husband and I thought we were moving here for one reason, but then later we realized God had led us here for a completely different reason. It didn't matter that the circumstances weren't what we expected when we came here. God used our limited knowledge to get us to the right place." She did not realize it, but the Lord was speaking through her; her comment applied to my situation as well.

God has often spoken to me through someone's sermon when one phrase has jumped out at me. I do not remember anything else about the message, but I can still clearly recall those words years later because they hit my heart with such impact that they changed my life.

The Lord will often speak as you read the Bible and a verse leaps out and grabs your heart. Someone once said, "I thought I was reading the Bible, but it turned out that the Bible was reading me." Whenever a verse hits you with conviction, the Holy Spirit is speaking to you in a personal way, giving you instructions to apply to your life.

If you want the Lord to continue speaking to you, you must obey what He has already revealed to you. Why would God keep giving you instructions if you have not done what He has already told you?

Some people have never figured out why they cannot hear the Lord's voice. It is simple. They are not willing to do what He says. After King Saul disobeyed God, he prayed for guidance but the Lord did not answer him (see 1 Samuel 14:37).

However, if you will faithfully obey what He has revealed to you, He will continue to give you more revelation. He speaks to those who will carry out His will.

Guidance Through Counselors

Another way the Lord can speak to you is through wise counselors. Many people will tell you the *wrong* things to do, which can cause you to make terrible decisions you will later regret. But God will use godly people to give you wise counsel so that you will make right decisions.

How can you know that you are listening to the correct advice? You must make sure that those who advise you meet certain qualifications. Jesus said, "Take care what you listen to" (Mark 4:24). Many people have offered me advice with ulterior motives, trying to manipulate me. Their hidden agenda distorted their advice and made it unreliable.

You will never have a shortage of people who love to tell you what to do. For this reason, you must use a filter to screen out the wrong counselors. Clara Null said, "If it's free, it's advice. If you pay for it, it's counseling. If you can use either one, it's a miracle." The true value of advice is determined by how much it helps you solve your problem.

We use air filters in our home air-conditioning units to keep dirt out. Our cars are fitted with fuel filters to screen out the impurities in gasoline. Even our computers use filters to block cookies, viruses and hackers. So why not use a filter to screen out terrible advice that can ruin your life?

One comedian quipped, "Anyone who is thinking about seeing a psychiatrist ought to have his head examined." Having a degree in counseling is not infallible proof that the individual will give you good, reliable advice. So how do you find the right experts who can help you make correct decisions?

Before you seek anyone's advice on a major decision, make sure your counselors exhibit the qualifications listed below. Someone has said, "An open mind is like an open window. It needs a screen to keep the bugs out." You also need to screen your counselors to keep out bad advice by doing three things.

1. *Choose advisors who walk closely with God*

The biblical prophets spoke words from God primarily to the people of Israel and Judah. But we also find other instances where the Lord used people to give specific instructions to others. God gave messages to Samuel to speak to Saul, Elisha to speak to Naaman, Nathan to speak to David, Agabus to speak to Paul, and Paul to speak to the centurion on a ship. The Lord used these men as His mouthpieces. They all had one thing in common—they were godly men who heard from God and delivered the correct message.

King David begins the book of Psalms with this bit of wisdom: "How blessed is the man who does not walk in the counsel of the wicked" (Psalm 1:1). Out of all the things he could have said, he did not want us to miss this important principle—*ignore the advice of ungodly people.* When it comes to ungodly counsel, just say no.

If the people who influence you do not know the Lord, they will often tell you things that do not line up with God's will. Their opinions can pressure you to make bad choices.

Years ago a pregnant woman went to see a doctor, who advised her to get an abortion. He told her that she would not live through childbirth and the baby would probably not survive either. She did not feel right about his diagnosis and ignored his counsel.

She did not have any complications giving birth to a healthy boy she named John. He grew up to be Dr. John Walvoord, the great theologian and author who was president of Dallas Theological Seminary for over thirty years. And what happened to John's mother? She lived to be over one hundred![1]

I know a man that I will call Ned, who attended a Christian youth camp when he was in high school. At the summer camp he gave his life to the Lord and felt that he was called to the ministry. For the first time, he believed that he had a purpose in life.

But soon after the summer ended, he quit reading his Bible and did not stay in fellowship with his Christian friends. It was not long before he drifted away from church and started listening to the wrong people.

Ned started partying and taking drugs with his friends. One evening he and his buddy drove to a prearranged meeting place to buy some dope. When the other car pulled up, his friend got out of the car to make the deal. An argument ensued, and then gunshots rang out. His acquaintance killed two people, and then he ran back to the vehicle. He jumped in the car, nervously waving the gun in his hand. He yelled at Ned to start driving. Ned panicked and drove the getaway car. Now he was an accomplice to murder! The police soon tracked them down and arrested them on murder charges.

I visited Ned in his jail cell as he was awaiting trial. He claimed he did not know that his friend would kill those two people in the drug deal. In spite of his claim of innocence, the jury found him guilty. Ned is now serving a 38-year prison sentence. He will be living most of the rest of his life behind bars because he foolishly chose to walk in the counsel of ungodly people.

The Lord told Israel not to associate with pagan nations "for they will surely turn your heart away after their gods" (1 Kings 11:2). This is not rocket science—hanging around the wrong people and listening to their advice will lead you down the wrong road. That is why it is so important to choose advisors who love God and have a track record of hearing His voice and making good decisions.

Does that mean that you can never have a non-Christian mechanic or financial counselor? It is not necessarily wrong, but it is risky if they are motivated by greed and want to rip you off. It is safer to hire a godly person who is honest and wants what is best for you.

A professional counselor told me that not all counselors want to see their patients get well. He knew colleagues who would string out the counseling for years to keep the income flowing in. One counseling patient said, "I must be the only guy who spent $10,000 on a couch and I still don't own it!" Unethical advisors will try to take advantage of those who are naive. On the other hand, godly counselors have pure motives without a hidden agenda. You can trust them.

2. Choose advisors who are knowledgeable and experienced

The first filter separates those who love the Lord and have integrity from those who do not. However, just because a person is a Christian does not mean he or she knows enough to give you advice. You must use a second filter to sort out the knowledgeable counselors from those who are not. It is typically not a good idea to choose friends to advise you just because they like you. Be selective and choose wise, experienced counselors who have already gone down the road you are about to journey on.

After King Solomon died, his son Rehoboam took his place. Rehoboam asked advice from the wise elders who had ruled with his father. They suggested that if he would be a servant to the people of Israel, lighten their workload and speak good words to them, they would respond in a positive way and would serve him forever.

Instead of listening to their recommendation, he turned to his friends that grew up with him for advice, even though they were inexperienced. They gave him the exact opposite counsel he had received from the elders, and advised him to make life hard on the people. Like a bully bragging about his toughness, they told him to say to the people, "My little finger is thicker than my father's loins. Whereas my father loaded you with a heavy yoke, I will add to your yoke; my father disciplined you with whips, but I will discipline you with scorpions" (1 Kings 12:10–11).

He ignored the wise counsel of the elders and followed his friends' foolish counsel instead, which led to a split in the kingdom.

It is not necessary to ask advice on every decision you make. No one needs to tell you what color socks to wear. You do not need to ask opinions for minor matters. But if you are facing a major decision, you could use some wise counsel.

King Solomon said, "For by wise guidance you will wage war" (Proverbs 24:6). Waging war is a major decision with enormous consequences. Making a mistake in strategy could cost thousands of lives.

A king who is planning to engage in war would be crazy to listen to advisors who have never been in the combat zone. They would not understand the enemy's strategy or what tactic to use to defeat them. The king would be wise to lean on the expertise of veteran military personnel who have been tested and have succeeded in the battlefield.

The same principle holds true with every other area where advice is needed—find people who are knowledgeable, experienced and wise in their respective fields. Search for the right person who understands the specific problem you are dealing with. If your house needs to be repaired, find a godly repairman who can fix your problem and will charge you a fair price. Your counselors should know what they are doing. Otherwise, how can they give you good advice?

I once went to a paint store to match some colors for my house. A young salesman who saw me looking at samples asked, "May I help you?"

While I was explaining how I wanted to match some colors in my house, I could not help but notice his clothes. He wore a red and blue wildly patterned shirt with some outdated checkered brown pants that did not match. If he did not know how to match his own clothes, why would I think that he could match the colors in my house?

If a counselor cannot successfully apply his advice to his own life, then it will not work for you either. If you are drowning, do not ask another drowning person to rescue you. You might be attracted to those who have the same problems as yours. They may even make you feel good through their sympathy because they know what you are going through. But they probably cannot help you *solve* your problem because they have not solved their own.

3. Choose advisors who care about what happens to you

A man in a café looked over the menu. "What'll you have today?" the waitress asked.

"I'll have the chicken casserole and a kind word."

A few minutes later the waitress returned and set his meal on the table.

"Where's the kind word?" the man asked.

The waitress leaned over and whispered, "Don't eat the chicken casserole."

Pick counselors who will tell you the truth, even if it is something you do not necessarily want to hear, like "Stay away from the chicken casserole." Your advisors should be genuinely concerned about what happens to you if you follow their advice.

When the apostle Paul traveled to Tyre, the disciples "kept telling Paul *through the Spirit* not to set foot in Jerusalem" (Acts 21:4). Paul had made up his mind that he was going to Jerusalem anyway.

The next day, when Paul arrived in Caesarea, the Lord sent the prophet Agabus to warn him that he would be bound and delivered to the Gentiles if he went to Jerusalem. Everyone, including his traveling companion Luke, begged him not to go. Prophets in two different cities delivered the same warning message to him.

You would think Paul would reconsider his decision. *Could the Lord be trying to tell me something?* Instead, Paul ignored their advice, stating that he was willing to die for Jesus (see Acts 21:9–14).

The real issue was not his willingness to die for his faith, but whether it was God's will for him to go there at that time. Because the disciples were telling him "through the Spirit," some Bible scholars believe Paul made a mistake in going.

Dr. Donald Barnhouse writes, "I firmly believe Paul was wrong in this. . . . Paul was determined to do things his way, no matter what God wanted."[2]

King Solomon said, "Faithful are the wounds of a friend, but deceitful are the kisses of an enemy" (Proverbs 27:6). The kisses of an enemy are flattering and manipulative words that may make you feel good but are spoken with a hidden motive. Your enemies actually want to see you fail; they will butter you up so that you will listen to their terrible suggestions.

If you are drowning, do not ask another drowning person to rescue you.

In contrast, some of the best advice I have received has come from the wounds of my friends. They have pointed out my blind spots—mistakes and weaknesses of which I was unaware. It is not easy to hear the painful truth from a friend.

The truth may hurt for a little while, but in the long run the wise advice will help you become a better person.

4. Choose a team of godly, wise and caring advisors

Two hobos, both destitute, were sitting on a park bench. One said, "I'm a man who never took advice from anybody." The other man stuck out his hand and said, "Shake, old buddy. I'm a man who followed everybody's advice."

The two biggest mistakes you can make are (1) not listening to anyone and (2) listening to everyone. The correct balance is somewhere between those two extremes.

Solomon gives another clue about making decisions. "In abundance of counselors there is victory" (Proverbs 24:6). Having a group of qualified advisors can help you make better decisions, so make sure that quality comes before quantity.

Gideon reduced the size of his army to get rid of his fearful and inattentive soldiers. You must disqualify all the ungodly, unknowledgeable and uncaring people from being on your advisory team.

Seek out spiritually mature, wise and caring counselors. Then ask several of them to advise you. Your goal is not to get a majority opinion, but for your selected group to share with you their expertise and wisdom. Preferably, each counselor is a specialist in a different area. Each one will see your problem from a different perspective and can point out things you may not have considered. By combining your own ideas with the wisdom of your counselors, you will see the big picture and will know how to proceed.

With major decisions, it is wise to get opinions from two or three of your qualified counselors. "Every fact is to be confirmed by the testimony of two or three witnesses" (2 Corinthians 13:1). If you need advice concerning a health situation, you do not need to call all of your advisors, but only the ones who are knowledgeable in the medical field. Likewise, if you need insight into raising children, you should call on wise parents of children older than yours. They can speak from experience about how they handled the problems their kids faced.

If your counselors receive their livelihood in their field of expertise, you should be willing to pay them for their advice. If they choose not to receive payment, it will be their decision and not yours. Depending on the situation, some advice will be free, but in cases of legal matters, your counselors should be paid. The help you receive will be well worth the money.

As the Scripture clearly states, the Lord can and will speak to you through other people. Even so, never forget that the responsibility for the actions you take falls on you and not on your counselors.

➡ LEARNING TO TRUST

1. Jesus said, "Take care what you listen to" (Mark 4:24). Why did He give this warning, and how does what we hear affect us either positively or negatively?

2. King David said you will be blessed if you do not follow the advice of evil people (see Psalm 1:1). What kind of blessing do you think he meant?

3. Why is it important to qualify your counselors before you let them advise you?

4. King Solomon said, "For by wise guidance you will wage war" (Proverbs 24:6). Why is it important to get advice from a wise, experienced person before you make a major decision?

9

Following Your Heart

It is the heart which perceives God and not the reason.

—Blaise Pascal

When I was a student at Texas A&M University, I was also a member of the Corps of Cadets, which is an ROTC program that trains college students to serve in the armed forces. I had planned to serve in the Air Force after college and possibly make the military my career. At the beginning of my junior year, I signed a contract with the Air Force which obligated me to serve eight years in the military after I graduated.

After receiving my degree from A&M and my Air Force commission, I was told to wait for my orders for my first assignment. During the waiting period, I felt a strong urge to enroll in a seminary for ministry training. That did not make sense because I would soon be leaving for pilot training. In my mind, Mr. Logic was screaming, *Are you crazy? How can you attend seminary for three years when you have an eight-year obligation with the Air Force? As soon as you receive that letter, you will have to drop out of school. You will waste a lot of money and look like a fool.*

Nevertheless, whenever I prayed, the desire in my heart to attend seminary became even stronger. I knew I needed to trust the Lord with my heart, even though what I was about to do made no sense (see Proverbs 3:5–6). I decided to follow where my heart was leading me. I sent in my application to Southwestern Baptist Theological Seminary just before classes were to begin.

When you are being led by the Holy Spirit, He will guide you through your heart.

At the time, I did not have enough money to pay for my first semester. I knew if God was truly leading me there, He would provide everything I needed. I packed up my car and drove to Fort Worth, Texas, to begin my journey in ministry.

After arriving, I found an apartment off campus and accepted a job as a janitor in the men's dorm, which provided the income I needed to squeak by. As I attended classes, I knew that God would have to perform a miracle for me to finish my education. Any day, I would receive that letter from the Air Force and would have to drop out of seminary.

Several weeks later, as expected, the letter came in the mail. To my surprise, it was not asking me to report for active duty. Instead, the letter offered to release me from my eight-year active duty obligation!

The Vietnam War had ended, which meant the Air Force did not need as many active duty officers. I could choose between fulfilling my eight-year military commitment in active duty, or I could serve ninety days active duty and then be inactive reserve for the rest of my eight years. That meant I could finish my three-year program in seminary.

I suddenly understood why God wanted me to follow that strong desire within me, even though it seemed like a crazy idea. I had no idea that the Air Force would offer me this option, but the Lord did. And that is why God communicated His will through such an intense pulling in my heart.

I chose to serve my ninety days during the summer between my first and second years in seminary. I received my master's degree in theology, which proved to be crucial to everything I would be doing in the future.

Following the desire in my heart proved to be right, even when logic told me it was wrong. My heart overruled my mind. The Lord provided for me in amazing ways and I paid for my education without ever having to borrow a dime.

As I looked back on the situation, God's guidance became abundantly clear. The Lord wanted to divert my steps in a new direction, so He planted the desire in my heart to pull me a different way. He was under no obligation to give me any additional information, but I had to trust Him when things did not make sense to me.

How the Holy Spirit Works in Your Heart

When you are being led by the Holy Spirit, He will guide you through your heart. "Following your heart" does not mean fulfilling your selfish impulses, but following the Holy Spirit's leading. He will never lead you to do something against the teachings of the Bible. The Holy Spirit can impress your heart in several different ways.

1. The Holy Spirit will act as the "wanter" inside your heart

Even people who do not know God will give the advice to "follow your heart." Left to itself, the heart will mislead you every time. The prophet Jeremiah said, "The heart is more deceitful than all else and is desperately sick; who can understand it?" (Jeremiah 17:9). "Following your heart" only applies after certain conditions have been met.

> When you surrender your will to Him, He changes your heart so that you will **want what He wants** you to do.

Be honest and examine your motives. It is easy to convince yourself that a wrong decision is actually the right one because you want your own way rather than God's. However, your heart can lead you down the right path when you choose to be controlled by the Holy Spirit.

Not long after I became a Christian, I started wondering what it meant to be selfish. My goal was to be "dead to self," and I thought that if I really loved God alone, I would not have any of my own desires. My twisted reasoning led me to wrongly believe that if I had any desires in my heart, they all must be selfish. I concluded that being "dead to self" meant I had to be miserable instead of enjoying life.

Since I was a new believer and did not understand many things about God's leading, I sought the advice of a mature Christian to clear up the matter for me. My friend explained that since I surrendered my life to Jesus, He would put desires inside my heart as a way to guide me. Since I had surrendered myself to do God's will, He would direct my steps through the desires in my heart.

The Holy Spirit is God's Spirit living inside of every Christian. The moment you trust Jesus as your Savior, His Spirit enters into your heart. The prophet Ezekiel prophesied to Israel: "I will give you a new heart and put a new spirit within you. . . . *I will put My Spirit within you and cause you to walk* in My statutes, and you will be careful to observe My ordinances" (Ezek. 36:26–27). The apostle Paul wrote, "[God] gave us *the Spirit in our hearts* as a pledge" (2 Corinthians 1:22). Again he says, "God has sent forth the *Spirit of His Son into our hearts*" (Galatians 4:6).

So now I not only have "me in me" but also "Christ in me" (see Romans 8:9; Colossians 1:27). I have two sets of desires inside: the desires of the Spirit, which are from God, and the desires of the flesh, which are my own. Paul writes, "Walk by the Spirit, and you will not carry out the desire of the flesh. For the flesh sets its desire against the Spirit, and the Spirit against the flesh; for these are in opposition to one another" (Galatians 5:16–17). These two sets of desires are constantly pulling you in different directions. You will only follow the desires of the Spirit when you have submitted yourself to His control.

It is not a normal desire to want to leave the comfort of America to serve as a missionary in Africa or India. Yet I have known people whose passion was to live in poverty-stricken countries to reach people for Christ. Where does that desire come from? It does not come from themselves, but from the Holy Spirit.

When you surrender your will to Him, He changes your heart so that you will *want what He wants* you to do. That is how He leads some people to go to Mongolia, while He tells others to be content and stay where they are right now. Do not assume that the Lord will always ask you to move somewhere else. Many people are trying to run away from their commitments, but they need to stay where they are to fulfill their obligations.

I have learned to follow the passion in my heart. If you will find your joy in pleasing the Lord, you are in a position where He can guide you through your heart. "Delight yourself in the LORD; and He will give you the desires of your heart" (Psalm 37:4). He will place a passion inside your heart so that you will want to obey what He wants you to do.

2. The Holy Spirit will tug at your heart

The Holy Spirit will lead you by pulling you in a certain direction. That is how He led me to seminary. The pull of the Holy Spirit can be compared to a little boy who was flying his kite. It flew so high that it rose into the clouds where he could not see it.

A man standing nearby tried to have some fun with him. He asked, "How do you know the kite is up there? Maybe it's gone. I can't see it. Can you?"

"No, I can't see it," the boy replied. "But I know it's up there because I can feel a little tug now and then."

The Holy Spirit will lead you by tugging at your heart in the direction you need to go. God's guidance is like a magnet that attracts you to do God's will and repels you away from places you should not be. But first you must be willing to be led.

George Mueller, an English evangelist in the 1800s, said to discover God's will, "I seek at the beginning to get my heart into such a state that it has no will of its own in a given matter. When you're ready to do the Lord's will, whatever it may be, nine-tenths of the difficulties are overcome."[1]

You must get to the place where you want God's will more than your own. Even Jesus surrendered His will to the Father by dying on the cross. He prayed in the Garden of Gethsemane, "My Father, if it is possible, let this cup pass from Me; yet not as I will, but as You will" (Matthew 26:39). Once your heart is in that place, the Lord can lead you without any hindrance or resistance from you.

3. The Holy Spirit will make His will "seem good" to you through an inner knowing in your heart

An "inner knowing" is not like a thought in your mind, but more like an intuition, an unmistakable *confidence* in your heart. Some people would call it a "gut feeling." One friend described it as, "You know that you know that you know."

The apostles and elders gathered together for the council at Jerusalem to determine the church's stance on circumcision. After much debate, they finally arrived at a position.

> It *seemed good* to the apostles and the elders, with the whole church, to choose men from among them to send to Antioch. . . . It *seemed good* to us, having become of one mind, to select men to send to you. . . . For it *seemed good to the Holy Spirit and to us* to lay upon you no greater burden.
>
> Acts 15:22, 25, 28

These church leaders were seeking God's will together. They carefully prayed and thought through their decision before they all felt right about it. Three times the Scripture mentions that "it seemed good."

Sometimes God confirms His will by what *seems* right. You can sense in your spirit it is the right thing to do. This assurance comes from the Holy Spirit bearing witness with your spirit. Again, just because something seems good to you does not mean it is always God saying yes. The elders thought through their decision and so should you.

4. The Holy Spirit will confirm His will through the peacefulness in your heart

Paul tells us, "Let the peace of Christ rule in your hearts." (Colossians 3:15). The Greek word for "rule" means "to act as an umpire" or "the one who decides." In sporting events, the umpire is the one who makes the decisions on close calls. He calls the baseball player safe or out, or the football player in bounds or out of bounds.

God's peace does the same thing; it makes the call concerning how to proceed. It works similar to a traffic light. If you are at total peace, it can be a green light telling you to go forward.

An unsettled spirit is a yellow light, telling you to be cautious. Inner turmoil can act like a red light, instructing you to stop. One thing is certain. The peace of the Lord can supernaturally calm your spirit, even in the middle of troubling circumstances. It is called "the peace of God, which surpasses all understanding" (Philippians 4:7 NKJV).

The Lord has given me incredible peace about some decisions I have made. At other times, I felt unsettled about a matter, which was God's way of saying I was headed in the wrong direction. When your peace is disrupted, the Holy Spirit could be warning you that something is not right.

Years ago, I decided to partner in ministry with another man. We were planning to meet at an attorney's office on a certain day to discuss incorporating the ministry. But the more I prayed about it, the more uncomfortable I became about joining him. My stomach was in turmoil. My uneasiness was about as far as I could get from "the peace that passes all understanding." It was as if God were yelling at me to stop the process.

I called my friend and told him I did not feel right about incorporating. He admitted, "Yeah, I'm not sure about it either." We cancelled the meeting with the attorney.

Later, I heard my friend had skipped town, leaving behind bills that he had not paid. I also found out he had been involved in immoral behavior that he had kept hidden. Although I had not known these things about this man, the Lord was aware of what was going on in secret. The reason God upset the peace in my heart was to keep me from making a horrible mistake.

Reasons You Might Lack Peace in Your Heart

A lack of peace does not necessarily mean that what you are praying about is not God's will. Other factors may be involved that will make you feel temporarily unsettled in your spirit.

This is for your good, just as stoplights protect you from getting into wrecks.

Lack of peace may mean it is God's will, but you need to get some questions answered first

Sometimes when you are making a decision, you have not done enough research about the situation. You still have too many unanswered questions. You probably need to do more investigation into the issues that are bugging you. Although you might not find every answer, if you can resolve most of your uncertainties, then God's peace will settle your heart so you can proceed.

Lack of peace may mean it is God's will, but the timing is not right

King Solomon said, "There is an appointed time for everything. And there is a time for every event under heaven. . . . He has made everything appropriate in its time" (Ecclesiastes 3:1, 11). At times the Lord will upset the peace in your heart because the timing of the situation is not right. It is like trying to pick a green peach off a tree. You need to delay your plan until it is ready to drop into your hands like a ripe peach.

Your lack of peace might be a sign from God to back off for a while. He may be arranging circumstances behind the scenes that are not apparent right now. After the people, events and other factors fall into place, the Holy Spirit will settle your spirit and prompt you to move forward.

Lack of peace may mean it is not God's will, and the Holy Spirit has removed your peace

If you are about to make a mistake, the Holy Spirit will remove the peace from your heart. Many people get angry with God when He tells them no. They think that He is withholding something good from them, but He is actually doing them a favor. When your spirit is in turmoil, think of it as a red traffic light to protect you.

In the jungles of eastern Sri Lanka, fifteen soldiers of a government commando unit were saved by two dogs they had adopted as mascots. The soldiers had completed a ten-mile hike when the dogs sensed danger. Running ahead toward a water hole where the unit planned to rest, the dogs suddenly began barking and circling the area. The troops carefully searched and discovered twelve buried grenades attached to a trigger wire. The soldiers did not know their lives were in danger until the dogs warned them by barking.[2]

But suppose those soldiers thought the barking of the dogs was just an annoyance that aggravated them. They would ignore the warnings, or maybe even try to silence the dogs. If the soldiers had not given heed to the dogs' barking, they might have been maimed or even killed. The dogs' yelping was actually the best way to signal danger to the soldiers.

When the Holy Spirit upsets the peace in your heart, you might get frustrated at first. However, it is actually the best way to warn you of impending danger. Do not get upset with God if this happens. Instead, be thankful. He is just trying to protect you from making a mistake that you will later regret.

➡ LEARNING TO TRUST

1. Read Proverbs 3:5–6. What does it mean to trust the Lord with your heart and to not lean on your own understanding?

2. The prophet Jeremiah said that the heart is deceitful above all else (see Jeremiah 17:9). What does he mean by this?

3. When you are born again, the Holy Spirit indwells your heart (see Galatians 4:6). In what ways will God lead you into truth through your heart?

4. What are three reasons that you may lack peace in your heart when you are making a decision?

10

Man's Rejection
Can Be God's Direction

You may not realize it when it happens, but a kick in
the teeth may be the best thing in the world for you.

—Walt Disney

During the Great Depression, Wallace Johnson, a dedicated
Christian, was devastated when he was fired from his job at a
sawmill. He and his wife desperately needed the income. Wallace felt that the world had caved in on him.

His worried wife asked, "What are we going to do?"

Wallace thought through his options and told her, "I'm going
to mortgage our home and go into the building business."

His first venture was constructing two small buildings. God
blessed his business with more construction projects. Within
five years, Wallace had become a multimillionaire and he later
founded the Holiday Inn motel chain.

In an interview, Wallace reflected on his life's journey. "Today, if I could locate the man who fired me, I would sincerely thank him for what he did. At the time it happened, I didn't understand why I was fired. Later I saw that it was God's unerring and wondrous plan to get me into the ways of His choosing."[1]

What looked like the worst thing that could happen to them was actually the best thing. This is just one of many examples where God used man's rejection as His direction. Through the Lord's amazing sovereignty, He can turn the curses of men into the blessings of God.

Think of rejection as a detour. You are driving down a familiar freeway and everything is going as planned. Then you see a sign that reads, "Bridge Is Out. Road Closed Ahead." Driving a little farther, you see another sign, "Take This Detour," which diverts you in another direction.

> Rejection is a common way that the Lord directs people to a new place.

This is going to mess up my schedule, you mutter under your breath as you pull off the highway.

Who wants to take a detour? Nobody. Now you are traveling down an unfamiliar road, hoping you will end up in the right place. You are upset with the change of plans, not to mention being inconvenienced.

But if you will think about it, those who sent you off the highway were actually doing you a favor. If you had kept going straight, you would have driven over a cliff! Although the detour came unexpectedly and created a hassle, you are much better off taking the new route instead of sticking with the old one.

Rejection works the same way. Maybe you have been faithfully working for a company for years. Then you find out the company has to downsize and chooses to keep an incompetent, inexperienced person, even though you are more qualified. You lose your job and suddenly find yourself on a detour, having to travel an unfamiliar road. Now you are worried about your future because you do not know what is next.

What is the right way to respond? Remember that trusting God forces out worry. You must choose to view your circumstances from the Lord's perspective.

Rejection from God's Point of View

Most people get furious when they are rejected and some even seek revenge on those who jilted them. If you were kicked out the door undeservedly, the sting is multiplied. Although you might not have chosen to be snubbed, you can choose how you will respond to it. If you get bitter and bad-mouth those who spurned you, it will only prolong your hurt and will place you in a position where God cannot bless you.

A much better option is to view your rejection as God's direction. In fact, rejection is a common way that the Lord directs people to a new place. When you submit yourself under His mighty hand, you give Him permission to use any means necessary to accomplish His purposes in your life. Sometimes the methods He uses can be painful, but they are for your own good.

Listed below are six truths about rejection that will help you see your situation from God's point of view.

Fact #1. God uses rejection to take you to a better place than your current situation

It is important to understand that the Lord may want to move you to a better place *without telling you ahead of time*. God knows the end from the beginning, but He is not obligated to tell you everything that is going to happen. This is where you must trust God that He has a better plan, instead of worrying about what will happen next.

> "For I am God, and there is no other; I am God, and there is no one like Me, declaring the end from the beginning, and from ancient times things which have not been done, saying, 'My purpose will be established, and I will accomplish all My good pleasure.'"
>
> Isaiah 46:9–10

Sometimes you can be drawn to a new job through the incentives of those who are trying to hire you. For example, a company offers to double your salary if you will leave your current position. At other times, you can be forced out of your job through slander and lies by those who dislike you. A co-worker might have given an untrue report to the powers that be, which resulted in the loss of your job. Or, perhaps you were laid off from your job due to the economic difficulties at your company.

Sometimes having the door slammed in your face is the only way you will change course.

I once served as an associate pastor on a large church staff that had to lay off employees due to the economy. The elders were forced to find ways to trim the budget, which meant cutting some staff positions. I had the least seniority, so I knew my position would go. When I received the news, I immediately knew in my spirit that God had something better in mind for me and that I would need to trust Him to take care of my family.

For months I sent out my résumé and patiently waited for a response. I found some temporary work to get by because ministers are not eligible for unemployment. I learned from personal experience what it felt like to be unemployed—and to trust Him to provide each day. A year later, the Lord opened a position for me that was a promotion and better in every way than what I had before.

It was a difficult year for me, but I can honestly tell you that I never worried during that time and the Lord always provided for our needs. Even though I loved my previous church, I thank God that I was laid off because He took me to a better place through His incredible sovereignty.

Why might God allow you to get laid off or fired? Because sometimes having the door slammed in your face is the only way you will change course. It may be that you are so comfortable in your present situation that you would never think about leaving on your own. Perhaps your loyal commitment keeps you there. You will just keep faithfully serving there forever, without any plans to leave. Your comfort zone keeps you from even considering that the Lord might have something better for you.

In that case, God will actually use rejection to interrupt your plans and send you in a new direction. He wants to take you to a different place that you would not have thought about going to on your own. It might not be until later, when you look back, that you will see God's hand in your situation. At that point, the light bulb comes on and you thank the Lord for allowing the painful experience. Unfortunately, it is hard to see God's hand at work when you are going through the traumatic situation. It is during the time of difficulty, when you are unsure of the outcome, that you must learn to trust in the sovereignty of God.

If you were unjustly fired from your job, you probably felt embarrassed, frustrated and humiliated. You wondered what you did to deserve the injustice and what the future held. You questioned whether or not God really understood what was going on. Why did He allow it? During those dark times, your faith was being tested to see if you really believed He has the best plans for you.

A friend of mine told me, "When I was fired from my job, it plunged me into depression and I wondered why God would allow such a thing. It turned out that getting fired was the best thing that ever could have happened to me! Not long after it happened, the Lord opened a door for the job that I've had for over twenty years, which I absolutely love. I thank God every time I think about the job that I lost because He had something much better planned for me. I couldn't see why He let it happen at the time, but it's real clear now as I look back. You don't know how many times I've thanked God that He let me get fired from my other job."

Fact #2. God chooses the players involved to make it happen

Another fact to understand about rejection is that God gets to pick the players who will carry it out—and these individuals may not be the ones that you would choose. It did not alarm Jesus one bit when Satan entered into His disciple Judas to betray Him (see Luke 22:3). The Lord often uses mean-spirited people as tools to accomplish His purposes, even though they are unaware of it.

In His infinite wisdom and sovereignty, God has the ability to overrule the evil intentions of others and turn their rejection of you around for your benefit. If Satan can take something good and turn it into evil, cannot God take something evil and turn it into good? Of course He can, but it is hard for us to comprehend what the Lord is doing when we are hurting.

> "'For My thoughts are not your thoughts, nor are your ways My ways,' declares the LORD. 'For as the heavens are higher than the earth, so are My ways higher than your ways and My thoughts than your thoughts.'"
>
> Isaiah 55:8–9

Maybe your spouse ran off with someone else. Perhaps your parents abused or abandoned you, which makes you feel worthless. God did not cause those incidents to happen, so He is not the one to blame. Take comfort in the fact that He still has a plan for your life, no matter what that person did to you. God will not immediately correct every injustice at the moment it happens, but promises that those who caused you harm will be held accountable on the Judgment Day. Until that day comes, you must let go of your pain and get on with your life.

What happened to you did not sabotage God's plan for you because He is able to write a better script for the remainder of your life. When Joseph's brothers threw him into a pit and sold him into slavery, God used their hateful actions as part of the script. Joseph did not get angry and bitter at his brothers for what they did to him. Instead, he fully submitted himself to divine providence, knowing that God would somehow use their malicious dealings to get him to a better place.

Joseph's hateful brothers never realized that they were merely pawns in a chess game with God. The Lord used their rejection to transport Joseph to Egypt, where he was promoted to a ruler. If his brothers had not sold him into slavery, Joseph's promotion would not have happened. He probably would have tended sheep until his dying day and would have never fulfilled his destiny. But God, foreknowing that his jealous siblings would reject him, chose to use their rejection as His direction through His amazing sovereignty. He overruled their scheme and can do the same for your situation, if you will keep trusting Him with the right attitude.

> If Satan can take something good and turn it into evil, cannot God take something evil and turn it into good?

Fact #3. Two different purposes are going on at the same time

After Joseph was reunited with his brothers, he said, "As for you, you meant evil against me, but God meant it for good" (Genesis 50:20). Did you catch the truth he revealed? Two different purposes were going on at the same time. The brothers were motivated by evil, but God outsmarted them and overruled their actions so that Joseph would be blessed in the end.

Jesus revealed two simultaneous plans in operation when He said, "But before all these things, they will lay their hands on you and *will persecute you,* delivering you to the synagogues and prisons, bringing you before kings and governors for My name's sake. *It will lead to an opportunity* for your testimony" (Luke 21:12–13). The persecutors thought they were putting the disciples on trial, but God was just using them to get His followers in the right place so they could preach to kings!

When Christ stood trial before Pontius Pilate, His destiny seemed to be in the Roman officer's hands. Pilate, wishing to show himself in charge, said to Jesus, "Do You not know that I have authority to release You, and I have authority to crucify You?" In response, Jesus revealed a remarkable insight about the sovereignty of God. He answered, "You would have no authority over Me, unless it had been given you from above" (John 19:10–11). He explained to Pilate that two different purposes were going on at the same time. Pilate could not do anything without God permitting it.

Jesus viewed the mock trial as part of a divine plan with a higher purpose. He knew His Father was in complete control, and that was why He was not squirming before Pilate and pleading for mercy. He could have said, "Mr. Pilate, I realize how powerful you are and I'm not quite sure My Father can do anything about it. Could you please give Me one more chance?

I promise I'll be good and won't make anyone else angry. I beg you to please let Me go!"

Jesus did not react in that way because He knew that His Father controls the world. He said earlier to the Jews, "Truly, truly, I say to you, the Son can do nothing of Himself, unless it is something He sees the Father doing; for whatever the Father does, these things the Son also does in like manner" (John 5:19).

When Jesus chose His disciples, the Father told Him to pick the man who would betray Him. Jesus did not erupt in protest, "Father, I can't believe that You had Me choose Judas to be My disciple. And then You had Me put him in charge of the money box? What *were* You thinking?"

Because Jesus always stuck to the Father's script, He never got offended—even when His disciples deserted Him. Jesus did not get angry when Peter denied Him. He did not say to him, "Peter, I can't believe that you denied Me three times after all the miracles you've seen Me do. Remember when you walked on the water to come to Me? Duh! Did you forget about catching that fish with the coin in its mouth to pay our taxes? What were the odds of *that* happening without My intervention? Don't you remember when I was transformed to glowing white on the mount of transfiguration, and you heard an audible voice from heaven saying that I was God's Son? How could you forget that?

"Peter, you cut off Malchus's ear with a sword in the Garden of Gethsemane. Guess who had to stick it back on his head? You're looking at Him, bub. And now you've turned into a chicken and have denied Me three times. I'm highly offended that you wouldn't even admit that you know Me. Peter, I'll never forgive you for that. Never!"

Jesus did not say that to Peter, nor was He offended by his rejection because He knew two purposes were in operation at the same time. He looked past what the little hands of men were doing and saw God's big hand overruling their actions.

You also need to see the Father's hand at work in your life, even when things are not going your way. God does not always let you in on what He is doing. Trust fills the gap when you do not understand.

Never forget that those who reject you do not realize they are pawns in God's hand. Although they intend to cause you harm through their rejection, the Lord will use them for another purpose to bring about something good.

Fact #4. God allows painful rejection so you will have no doubt it is time to move on

You usually transition to another place in a couple of ways. You can willingly move to a new place by your own choosing, or you can be forced out against your will by the decisions of others. The first way is usually pleasant. The second way is painful.

The sting of rejection hurts. It makes you feel *un*wanted, *un*loved and *un*appreciated. Often the snubbing is *un*fair and *un*called for.

But you need to add one more "un" to the equation. You must *un*derstand that rejection is one of God's tools to maneuver people to a new place. It is hard to comprehend how a good God can use evil people. And it is even more difficult to see God's purpose when you are writhing in agony. The sting of rejection is devastating and hurts deeply. But God allows you to experience the pain so you will have no doubt that it is time to move on and not look back with regrets. Rejection can actually be God's protection when He stops a relationship to protect you from being hurt worse in the future.

Perhaps someone you deeply love turns their back and leaves you. Your fiancé broke off your engagement and the rejection is killing you. Your whole world has come crashing down and you think you cannot go on. But it may be that God has allowed your crisis because He has someone better reserved for you.

Whenever people are devastated from a broken engagement, I tell them, "Although you can't see it right now, this is a huge blessing in disguise. God has just spared you from a lifetime of grief through a short time of pain. He has something better planned for you although you cannot see it right now."

One of my friends told me that when his fiancée broke off their engagement, it was the most painful thing he had ever experienced. He plunged into deep depression and thought he would never pull out of it. But then something happened. He said, "About three months later I saw the most beautiful woman I had ever laid my eyes on. When I saw her, I completely forgot about that other girl. I knew she was the one for me. We've now been happily married over thirty years. God knew that I had to completely let go of the wrong person so I could find the right one. Every time I think about it, I thank God that I didn't marry the other gal!"

Fact #5. To keep the right attitude, you must focus on God's hand and not on how the other person hurt you

> God does not always let you in on what He is doing. Trust fills the gap when you do not understand.

> Rejection can actually be God's protection when He stops a relationship to protect you from being hurt worse in the future.

You must choose to focus your attention on the hand of God. Choose to look past your devastation and see what the Lord wants to do. If you will focus on His purpose and not the evil motives of others, you will become thankful instead of bitter.

Wouldn't it be wonderful to view every circumstance as God sees it? The Lord knows what you are going through right now. It helps to have "eyes that see," which means to have God's perspective as you walk through life. Only through the eyes of faith can you be confident that He is in control of your circumstances.

> Although you might not see it until later, those who reject you are actually doing you a huge favor.

As you walk in the footsteps of Jesus, you will share the same painful experiences that He went through. He told His disciples, "'A slave is not greater than his master.' If they persecuted Me, they will also persecute you" (John 15:20). Just as He was rejected, so you will be too. All the prophets were rejected for doing God's will. Why do you think it would be different for you?

A pastor who had faithfully served his church for many years shared about the rejection he felt when two elders forced him out:

> After I announced my resignation, the church held a farewell party for my wife and me. Ninety-nine percent of the congregation hugged us, cried, and told us how much they appreciated what we had done for them. However, it bothered me that two elders were glad to see me go. One of them did not even speak to me the entire evening. They had purposely kept my salary low, which was part of the reason I knew it was time for me to move on to a different place.
>
> I would be lying if I told you their rejection did not hurt. I could not understand how these two church leaders could be so mean to me after I had cared for their families so many times over the years.
>
> The next day, as I was cleaning out my desk at the church, I noticed a piece of paper in the bottom of a drawer. The memo contained some scribbled notes from a sermon I had prepared

four years earlier. For some reason this scrap of paper had slipped to the bottom of the drawer without my noticing it. The sermon was on "Rejection."

On the paper was a list of verses that I had jotted down. Every verse had been scratched out except one. I stared at the one verse on the paper that was left: "And He began to teach them that the Son of Man must suffer many things and *be rejected by the elders* and the chief priests and the scribes, and be killed, and after three days rise again" (Mark 8:31).

The words "rejected by the elders" jumped off the page. I had never thought about that part of the verse before. I suddenly realized I was following in His footsteps. Jesus was rejected by stubborn elders, so it was okay for me to also be rejected by callous elders.

I do not have any doubt that God let me find that piece of paper with the Scripture at that moment to speak to my situation. Years have passed since that incident happened, and my wife and I smile whenever we think about it. Although we could not see anything positive in their rejection at the time, the elders were actually doing us a great favor. The Lord used their rejection to not only take us to a much nicer place to live with a better salary, but we have reached far more people for the Lord than we could have if we had stayed there. It was worth going through a few moments of painful rejection to get us to a much better place.

I will say it again—choose to see your rejection from God's point of view and look forward to the good future He has planned for you.

Fact #6. God finishes the script by turning the curse into a blessing

God turned the horrible crucifixion of Jesus into the salvation plan for the entire world. He took the rejected stone and sculpted Him into the foundation stone for the Church. Jesus quoted the Psalms, saying, "The stone which the builders rejected, this became the chief corner stone; this came about from the Lord, and it is marvelous in our eyes" (Matthew 21:42; see Psalm 118:22–23).

In this passage we see God's big hand overruling the evil little hands. "This came about from the Lord" shows that God permits rejection to happen. "And it is marvelous in our eyes" means that the Lord turns rejections into blessings—and you will see it.

What the Father did for Jesus, He will also do for you. Because God loves you, He will make sure that their curse is turned into your blessing. "The LORD your *God turned the curse into a blessing for you because the* LORD *your God loves you*" (Deuteronomy 23:5). God is in charge and He is able to make the rest of your life better than ever before.

If you have been rejected, rest assured that the Lord still has a good plan for your life. He has a different perspective than anyone on earth: "And coming to Him as to a living stone which has been *rejected by men, but is choice and precious in the sight of God*" (1 Peter 2:4).

So choose to view your rejections from God's perspective. He may be protecting you from future harm. He may halt a relationship so He can guide you to His choice for you. Failure to be hired for a job may mean God is directing you to a different assignment. Submit yourself to the lordship of Jesus Christ and He will make sure that you are not disappointed.

➡ LEARNING TO TRUST

1. After Joseph was reunited with his brothers, he said, "As for you, you meant evil against me, but God meant it for good" (Genesis 50:20). What does it mean that two different purposes are going on at the same time? (See Luke 21:12–13.)

2. Why is it important to view rejection from God's perspective rather than focusing on what people did to you?

3. Jesus was talking about Himself when He said, "The stone which the builders rejected, this became the chief corner stone; this came about from the Lord, and it is marvelous in our eyes" (Matthew 21:42). How did Jesus view His rejection by the religious leaders? What does "and it is marvelous in our eyes" mean?

4. Deuteronomy 23:5 says, "The LORD your God turned the curse into a blessing for you because the LORD your God loves you." How does this apply when you are rejected by people who hate you? Why does God do this for you?

11

Open and Closed Doors

The reason so many people never get anywhere in
life is because when opportunity knocks, they are
out in the backyard looking for four-leaf clovers.
—Walter P. Chrysler

Sometimes guidance begins *from the inside* when the Lord
puts thoughts in your mind and desires in your heart. At other
times, guidance starts *from the outside* when your circumstances
change. God may point you in a new direction by opening a
door of opportunity, or by closing a door of potential disaster.

An open door is when circumstances open up for you to
venture in a new direction. It could be a job offer, a buyer for
your home, a proposal to get married, a promotion to a higher
position, a request to move to a new place, or an invitation to
join an organization.

But God will also guide you by closing doors. A shut door
is when circumstances keep you from proceeding. Maybe a

business deal falls through, a promise turns into a shattered dream, or a relationship comes to an end.

A closed door usually forces you to stop and reconsider your options. You must look in a new direction—to a place you would never have chosen on your own, as has been discussed in the previous chapter. The Lord closes doors for good reasons. It might be to stop you from making a bad decision, to protect you from harm, or to point you to a better opportunity.

> Temptation will present itself as an open door, when it is actually a trap door.

Not every open door is God saying yes, and not every closed door is God saying no. However, when He wants you to do something, He will eventually open the door for you. If a door remains closed, sometimes you must keep knocking until it opens.

When Doors Are Open

If you believe that God rules from heaven, then you also understand that He can control your circumstances. He has the ability to open and close doors. The apostle John wrote, "This is what the One who is holy and true, who holds the key of David, says. *When he opens a door, no one can close it.* And when *he closes it, no one can open it.* I know what you do. *I have put an open door before you, which no one can close.* I know you have little strength, but you have obeyed my teaching and were not afraid to speak my name" (Revelation 3:7–8 NCV). God can open opportunities for anyone who keeps His Word.

When a door of opportunity opens it can be thrilling, but it can also be scary. Fear is the traveling companion that accompanies every opportunity. When it looks like you are finally going to get a break, fear shows up to talk you out of it!

A new opportunity will challenge you to break out of your normal routine and will make you feel uncomfortable at first. Fear can keep you trapped inside your comfort zone, which is the reason why many people do not answer the door when opportunity knocks.

You cannot let your fears keep you from doing God's will. If the Lord has opened a door for you, then He will give you the ability to handle whatever He is leading you to do. The *God factor* always deactivates the *fear factor* as you take steps of faith into the new adventure.

The Lord will call you to make many changes during your life. You might need to move to an unfamiliar city, change careers, or enter a new relationship. But He might also tell you to remain in your present situation when you want to run away from it. Too many people want to change seats simply because they are discontented, and not because the Lord is leading them.

Not every open door is an opportunity sent from God. Temptation will present itself as an open door, when it is actually a trap door. Satan loves to deceive people and lead them down the wrong paths. Avoid any unethical or immoral opportunity that will cause you to compromise your integrity.

Perhaps you want to walk through an open door, but the Holy Spirit keeps pulling back the reins. You have a hesitation in your spirit. Your lack of peace is usually the Holy Spirit's sign to wait. Remember that God's Word, the open door and the confirmation by the Holy Spirit must all be in harmony. If they are not, you are in danger of making a wrong decision.

> Not every open door is God saying yes, and not every closed door is God saying no.

When Doors Are Closed

If you sense that God's blessing is behind a closed door, you must keep knocking until the door opens. Many people get tired of knocking on doors and lose hope, but Jesus said to be persistent. "Keep asking, and it will be given to you. Keep searching, and you will find. Keep knocking, and the door will be opened to you" (Luke 11:9 HCSB).

Jesus instructed His disciples to pray at all times and not to give up or lose heart (see Luke 18:1). Since He is the One who answers your prayers, it would be wise to listen to His instructions. Persistent knocking is required for some doors to open.

> Focus your attention on the ability of God instead of the difficulty of the task.

Even if your situation looks impossible, keep asking. Even when you cannot understand how the door will open, keep knocking. You do not have to understand how the door will open. It will be difficult for you to have faith if you continue to wonder *how* God controls your circumstances. You will never be able to figure it out because His ways are beyond your understanding.

You must quit asking yourself, "*How* is it possible? *How* can God do it? *How* does He get people to change their minds?" Let God take care of that.

When the blind man asked Jesus to heal him, he did not say, "Before You heal me, could You please first explain exactly how You are going to do this miracle? It's a problem with my optic nerve, isn't it? Since You aren't performing surgery, and I don't see any scalpel, how do You plan to get in there to repair my eyeball?"

Jesus didn't say, "Those are great questions. Here is how I plan to heal you. . . ."

Instead of wondering *how*, start thinking *who*. Concentrate on God, who can do the impossible. Focus your attention on the ability of God instead of the difficulty of the task.

God can cause the door to open through someone you know, a committee choosing you over other candidates, or a divine appointment where you meet a person at just the right time. He can bring a buyer for your house. He can cause your résumé to grab the attention of the person in charge of hiring so that you will get the job instead of someone else.

If you have to move to another city, you may need God to open two doors. One door is a new job, while the other is someone to buy your house. But which comes first—accepting the job or selling the house?

Normally, it is best to first get hired at a new job before selling your home. But it does not always work out that way. What if the Lord brings a buyer for your house before you have secured that job? If you absolutely need to free yourself from your home mortgage, it might be wise to sell your home and then figure out where you can temporarily move.

I have normally been hired for a new job before I have sold my home. But one time I had to reverse the order. The Lord brought a buyer for my house, so I sold it before I found a job. Whether you get the job first and then sell your home to relocate or the other way around, it will require you to trust the Lord to make it happen. Only the Holy Spirit can show you the right order, which is sometimes determined by which door opens first.

How do you know when God wants you to move? It might be through a door opening that calls you to another place. It could be a desire in your heart that keeps pulling you to a certain location, or a thought that continues to echo in your mind. The Lord is not locked into one way of leading you. If you are married, make sure your spouse is in agreement with whatever you decide to do.

God's guidance does not always look the same. Every situation is unique and the Lord has a different plan for everyone. If you are completely yielded to Him as a horse is to its rider, He promises to lead you in making the right decisions.

Knocking on Doors

Do you need to find a job? Then don't just stand there, do something. Knock on doors and ask God to open the right opportunity. Explore all avenues because you do not know which one the Lord will choose to work through. Research job websites on the Internet and look in newspapers. Send out résumés. Make phone calls. Ask your friends and acquaintances if they know of employment opportunities. Fill out job application forms, in person if possible. You are more likely to get hired if you apply in person. A personal introduction shows a greater interest than sending an application through email.

I know a man who filled out dozens of online job applications but no one called him. Finally, he printed his résumé, visited several places where he had applied and handed it personally to the human resource directors. He received two job offers that day!

Do not send your résumé for every possible job opening, but apply for those jobs where you are qualified. If you are applying for that brain surgeon's job in the classified ads, it is unlikely you will get hired if you made a D in biology and never graduated from medical school. Do you get the point? You need to apply for those jobs where you are a match and have some knowledge and experience in that field.

Closed doors can be aggravating. Don't get discouraged when doors do not immediately open for you. If you will remember that the Lord only wants the best for you, it will keep you from worrying and being frustrated.

Reasons Doors Remain Closed

What if you keep knocking on a door but nothing happens? It may mean that the Lord does not want it to open. He may keep a door closed for several reasons.

1. A closed door can stop you from making a wrong decision

If you are about to make a bad decision, God may close a door to stop you. But you can ignore the warning, as was the case of Balaam in the Old Testament.

Balak, the king of Moab, wanted to hire the prophet Balaam to pronounce a curse on his enemy, Israel. As Balaam journeyed to Moab, the Lord sent an angel to stand in the path to block his way. His donkey saw the angel with his drawn sword in hand and turned away to protect Balaam from harm. Rather than heeding the warning, Balaam beat his donkey to force her back on the path.

Again, the angel stood in a narrow path with a wall on each side. When the donkey saw the angel, she pressed herself against the wall, which squeezed Balaam's foot. Still not getting the message, the prophet struck the donkey one more time.

As they went a little further, the angel positioned himself in a place where the donkey could not turn to the right or left. This time the donkey laid down. Balaam was furious and beat her again with his stick.

The Lord opened Balaam's eyes to see the angel with the drawn sword in his hand, so Balaam bowed to the ground. The angel said, "Behold, I have come out as an adversary, *because your way was contrary to me.* But the donkey saw me and turned aside from me these three times. If she had not turned aside from me, I would surely have killed you just now, and let her live" (Numbers 22:32–33). The compromise Balaam made was so detestable that this incident is mentioned in eight different books of the Bible.[1]

God will sometimes set up a roadblock for your own good. It may be a parent forbidding a teenager to associate with a questionable person or group. It could be a business deal that falls through, which would have brought a lawsuit. If you ignore the warning, you will suffer the consequences.

2. A closed door may protect you from danger

God closes some doors because He knows danger lies on the other side. The shut door protects you from getting hurt.

Suppose you see a door with a sign that reads, "Enter here for riches and success." Although you do not know what is behind the door, the sign looks appealing to you. You are ignorant of the fact that a vicious dog waits on the other side. If you open the door, the animal will rip you apart.

Be just as thankful for closed doors as open doors.

Before you grab the doorknob, a trusted friend stops you. "Don't open that door!" she warns. "I know what's on the other side, and the sign is deceiving you. Just trust me. You don't want to go through that door."

Now you have a decision to make. Should you open the door that looks so inviting, or do you heed your friend's warning? The opportunity seems too good to pass up, but your friend has never lied to you before.

When God shuts a door that you want to open, you must trust that He knows what lies behind the door and how it would harm you. He is not warning you because He is your enemy, but because He is your friend.

In what ways will the Lord close a door? He may arrange circumstances to block the way, or warn you through a lack of peace in your heart. Perhaps you can hear the growling coming from behind the door and have figured it out. The Lord wants you to turn away from it for your own good.

Think how many times you have been angry at a closed door, only to find out later it actually protected you from devastation. Behind that door might have been a dangerous relationship, or an unwise investment that would have wiped you out financially. It may have been a job that looked great on paper but would have made you miserable if you had accepted it.

God shuts doors to protect you from danger on other side. Since the Lord knows the future, you must trust Him to open the right doors for you and close the wrong ones.

3. A closed door can point you in a different direction

The apostle Paul kept running into closed doors on one of his missionary journeys. As he passed through the Galatian region, the Holy Spirit stopped him from going into Asia. From there he headed in a different direction toward Bithynia, but again the Lord shut the door. Paul was not sure what the Lord was trying to tell him.

That night he dreamed about a man in Macedonia calling for him to come over and help. Paul concluded that the Lord had opened the door to Macedonia, which was where he went to preach (see Acts 16:6–10). God directed Paul to the right place by closing two doors and then pointing him in another direction through a dream.

A closed door can indicate that God has a different plan in mind. If you are truly seeking to do God's will, be just as thankful for closed doors as open doors.

You read in a previous chapter about the church member who had a dream about where our new church would be built. A few years before that dream, another church in town had dwindled down to only a handful of members. The church had not paid the mortgage payments for nearly two years and was about to go into foreclosure. The building was in a great location with a main roadway near the property.

Our church approached them about purchasing their building, which would have prevented the foreclosure. We offered to assume their mortgage, pay their delinquent payments and give them a generous amount of money to start anew somewhere else. On paper, it looked like the perfect solution for both congregations.

Because the other church did not have a pastor, a stubborn woman had assumed control of the church. After we made our proposal, she never returned our phone calls. Instead of talking with us, she decided to sell the building to someone else.

When I received the news I was crushed. I could not understand why the Lord would close this door on us, yet open it for someone else.

The next Sunday, I spoke completely by faith to our congregation. "God has closed the door to buy that church building that we had been praying for. I believe He's going to provide a much larger piece of property for us. We will build a church over twice as large as the one we wanted to purchase."

It took a few years for me to understand why God had not granted our request. Our congregation had nearly tripled in size. The church building we had desperately wanted would have been too small for our growing numbers. The Lord opened a door for us to purchase land that was five times larger than the other property. We constructed a debt-free building nearly three times larger than the other church building.

What happened to the church building we originally wanted? By this time, other buildings had been constructed around it, which made it nearly invisible. The main entry road to the church had been closed, and the only way to get there was a roundabout way through a neighborhood. What looked like a great location a few years before became the worst possible site to have a church building!

God did us a huge favor by shutting that door, even though we were disappointed and confused at the time. Closed doors can be blessings in disguise, and the only way to accept this truth is by faith.

Now you know that a closed door is not necessarily bad news. Although you might not understand it now, you will look back and see things in a different light later.

➡ LEARNING TO TRUST

1. What does Revelation 3:7–8 tell us about the ability of God to open and close doors for us?

2. A closed door does not necessarily mean it is not God's will for you. If you believe it is God's will for the closed door to eventually open, what did Jesus say to do? (See Luke 11:9; 18:1.)

3. What are three reasons why the Lord might not open a door?

4. How did God use closed doors to divert the apostle Paul to the right place? (See Acts 16:6–10.)

12

Pay Attention to the Signs

If only God would give me some clear sign. Like making a large deposit in my name in a Swiss bank. If He would just speak to me once, anything, one sentence, two words. If He would just cough.

—Woody Allen

In the comedy film *The Man with Two Brains*, actor Steve Martin plays a brain surgeon whose wife has just died. He quickly falls in love with a devious gold digger who is only after his money. Martin stands in front of a portrait of his deceased wife and asks, "If there is anything wrong with my feelings for Dolores, just give me a sign. Any sign at all."

Immediately the picture starts spinning around, the room begins shaking, lights are flashing on and off and a voice screams, "No! . . . No! . . . No! . . . Noooooo!"

After everything settles back to normal, he says, "Just any kind of sign. I'll keep on the lookout for it."

In the next scene, he is standing at the altar with Dolores, saying, "I do."

Some people pay no attention to the signs. Every day we see signs that tell us what to do. A *Stop* sign tells us when to hit the brakes. The *Yield* sign says to let others have their way. *No U-Turn* means no turning back. A *Slow* sign instructs us to proceed with caution. The signs are placed at those locations for our own protection, and eventually we will suffer the consequences if we choose to ignore them.

In the spiritual realm, God also uses signs to point you in the right direction. Since He is in control of all things, He manages the circumstances in your life to show you whether or not you are on the right track. As you have already seen, rejection is a *Detour* sign to redirect you to a new place. God gives you a *No U-Turn* sign when you are tempted to return to a forbidden place. More often than not, He will show you a *Yield* sign when you need to humble yourself and let others have their way.

Another kind of sign is when God does something in a highly unusual way to confirm His will. Moses, Hezekiah, Gideon and others in the Bible all received miraculous signs of affirmation. Sometimes God initiated the signs, while at other times people asked God for them. If the Lord gave you a sign, would you recognize it?

There is a story about a Christian man who was afraid to share his faith. He prayed, "Lord, if you want me to share my faith with someone today, please give me a sign so I'll know who it is." As he was riding on a bus to work that day, a man sat down next to him.

He prayed, "Lord, is this the man I'm supposed to talk to, or is it someone else on the bus? Give me a sign."

At the next stop, everyone else got off the bus except the man seated next to him. Immediately the stranger started weeping, crying out with a loud voice, "I need to be saved! I'm a lost sinner, I need the Lord and I just need someone to tell me how to be saved!"

The Christian man bowed his head and prayed, "Lord, is this the sign, or should I look for another after I get off the bus?"

When the Lord flashes an unmistakable sign before your eyes, do not look for another confirmation. God's signs are not that difficult to figure out.

Asking God for a Sign

When Saul's son Jonathan was preparing to fight the Philistines, he looked for a sign that God would be with him. He told his armor bearer, "If they say to us, 'Wait until we come to you'; then we will stand in our place and not go up to them. But if they say, 'Come up to us,' then we will go up, for the LORD has given them into our hands; and *this shall be the sign to us*" (1 Samuel 14:9–10). God revealed this sign to him so that he would know how to respond to bring victory.

> A sign is when God does something in a highly unusual way to confirm His will.

We find many times in God's Word that the Lord gave people signs to confirm His will. The Lord spoke to King Ahaz saying, "Ask a sign for yourself from the LORD your God; make it deep as Sheol or high as heaven." Ahaz replied, "I will not ask, nor will I test the Lord!" (Isaiah 7:11–12).

The king turned down God's offer to ask Him for a sign because he thought he would be putting the Lord to the test. Ahaz failed to realize that not every request for a sign is an attempt to test God. In fact, a sign from God can have the reverse effect—putting your own faith to the test.

The Lord gave Ahaz a sign anyway: "Behold, a virgin will be with child and bear a son, and she will call his name Immanuel"

(Isaiah 7:14). This sign was fulfilled in the virgin Mary's miraculous conception and the birth of the Son of God.

A sign can be as simple as a door of opportunity opening or as complex as a set of circumstances miraculously coming together. Keep in mind that asking for a sign should not be your primary way of discovering God's will. Many times the fulfillment of a sign is accompanied with a difficult task, such as Gideon going into battle severely outnumbered.

1. Gideon asked for a wet fleece as a sign

Perhaps the most familiar "sign story" in the Bible is Gideon putting out a fleece of wool so he would know God's will. He was beating out wheat in the winepress when suddenly an angel appeared to give him a message—the Lord had chosen him to lead Israel to defeat the Midianites (see Judges 6).

> Signs are often followed by a severe testing of faith.

Even though Gideon knew he was talking to an angel, he was not so sure that he wanted to lead the charge into battle. To make certain that God had sent the message, he asked for a miraculous sign. The angel granted his request. He caused fire to come from a rock, which consumed some meat and bread, and then the angel disappeared.

You would think that would have been enough proof, but apparently Gideon was still not convinced. He wanted further proof from God. Gideon put a fleece of wool on the threshing floor and asked the Lord to send dew on the fleece, but let the ground around it remain dry. If God would just make that happen, Gideon said, "Then I will know that you will deliver Israel through me" (Judges 6:37).

The next morning, the fleece was wet and the ground dry. Gideon probably thought, *This is what normally happens.*

Naturally, the fleece would hold the water. So Gideon asked another sign, requesting that God would do just the opposite. He wanted the fleece to be dry and the ground wet.

Again, the next morning the Lord granted his request by making the fleece dry. God had now given Gideon four signs. He had sent an angel to miraculously appear, produced fire from a rock and passed two fleece tests. Gideon was finally convinced that the Lord would lead him to victory in battle.

Although it may be assuring to have solid proof like these confirmations, signs are often followed by a severe testing of faith. Gideon had to go fight the mighty Midianites with his army whittled down to just three hundred men. If you are planning to ask God for a sign of confirmation, be prepared to have your faith tested.

I would not advise doing what I am about to tell you, but I must confess that it is true.

A few months after I had met my future wife, Cindy, I wondered if she was the one God had picked out for me. When I asked the Lord about this, I believe He told me that she was indeed "the one." I wanted more proof, so I asked Him to confirm it with a sign. I prayed, "Lord, I'm going to put my finger down in the Bible and I would like you to speak to me through that verse about whether or not you have chosen Cindy to be my wife."

I shut my eyes, randomly flipped open my Bible and put my finger on Genesis 29:19. I peeked at the verse and could hardly believe my eyes. The passage was a quote from Laban when he gave his daughter to marry Jacob. He said, "It is better that I give her to you than to give her to another man."

What are the odds my finger would land on that Scripture? If God were going to give me a sign that Cindy was the one for me, that would be the perfect verse. I knew without a doubt that the Lord had confirmed His will.

Not long after this, my faith was tested in a way I was not expecting. We broke up! She wanted to date other people, so we went our separate ways. It broke my heart because deep down I knew she was meant to be my wife. We went several months without seeing each other or talking. The schools we were attending were hundreds of miles apart. With each passing day, it looked as though it was over for good.

Every day I prayed that God would bring her back to me. Whenever I started to doubt, I reminded the Lord about the verse that I had placed my finger on, "It is better that I give her to you than to give her to another man." God had given me that sign of confirmation because He knew I needed to keep trusting Him, no matter how bleak the circumstances appeared. The passage was the only hope I could cling to.

One day I received a letter from Cindy saying she was coming to town. I was thrilled to find out that God had changed her heart and she wanted to get back together!

I realized that God had a purpose for our breakup. During the time we were separated, the Lord refined our faith as we both grew closer to Him. Then He brought us back together and our relationship was established on a much stronger foundation to prepare us for marriage.

On our wedding day, the sign He had given me was fulfilled, and we have lived happily ever after. Over the years, I have told God hundreds of times, *Lord, thank You for giving her to me rather than any other man.*

Again, I would never suggest that you close your eyes and stick your finger in the Bible. It is highly unusual for the Lord to speak in that way.

2. Abraham's servant asked for a camel-watering sign

Abraham sent his servant out to find a wife for his son Isaac. The servant took ten camels with him and traveled hundreds of miles to Mesopotamia. He realized the importance of his responsibility and could not afford to make a mistake, so he asked God for a sign to confirm His will (see Genesis 24).

But what kind of sign should he ask for? It needed to be something extremely difficult, an act that would require divine intervention. The servant decided to ask that Isaac's appointed spouse would offer to water his camels for him.

> He said, "O LORD, the God of my master Abraham, please grant me success today, and show lovingkindness to my master Abraham. Behold, I am standing by the spring, and the daughters of the men of the city are coming out to draw water; now may it be that the girl to whom I say, 'Please let down your jar so that I may drink,' and who answers, 'Drink, and I will water your camels also'—may she be the one whom You have appointed for Your servant Isaac; and by this I will know that You have shown lovingkindness to my master."
>
> Genesis 24:12–14

For those of us who drive cars, that sign does not sound too miraculous. But if you had lived back then, you would have understood how ridiculous that request was. Abraham's servant brought ten camels with him, and each camel could drink up to thirty gallons of water. That meant whoever volunteered for the chore would have to draw *three hundred gallons* from the well to water his camels. It would be an exhausting task, requiring a tremendous amount of energy. What sort of person would be so gracious as to sacrifice several hours to do such grueling work for a stranger?

Immediately after he asked for the sign, the Lord led Rebekah to come to the well and offer to water his camels. She even said the exact words that the servant had requested from God as a sign, proving she was the wife appointed for Isaac.

Abraham's servant had asked for a highly unusual sign and the Lord answered by bringing the right woman to him. We know that

God made this happen because Jesus was a descendant of Isaac and Rebekah. If the Lord could arrange a divine appointment like this for Isaac, He can certainly do it for anyone else as well.

3. Hezekiah asked for a sign that the Lord would heal him

When King Hezekiah was gravely ill, he asked the Lord to give him more time to live. God sent the prophet Isaiah to announce that he would be given an additional fifteen years of life on earth. The king asked for a miraculous sign that the Lord would heal him, so Isaiah told him that the shadow on his stairway would go back ten steps (see 2 Kings 20:1–11). Turning back the shadow depicted the turning back of the clock in Hezekiah's life.

Perhaps Hezekiah should have left well enough alone and just died when his time came. After his life was extended, he made a foolish mistake. When the king of Babylon sent representatives to him, Hezekiah opened up his treasure house and showed them all his gold, silver and other valuable items. The prophet Isaiah was upset when he found out what Hezekiah had done. He prophesied that the days would come when the treasures he had shown them would be carried away to Babylon and his future children would be taken into captivity (see 2 Kings 20:12–18). This prophecy did come to pass, just as Isaiah had foretold.

But that was not the only problem created by extending Hezekiah's life. During his extra years of life, he had a son named Manasseh, who became king after he died. Manasseh was an evil king, rebuilding the high places and altars to false gods that Hezekiah had torn down. He even erected pagan altars in the temple, practiced witchcraft and sacrificed his own son to a pagan god (see 2 Kings 21:1–6). According to Jewish tradition, Manasseh murdered the prophet Isaiah by sawing him in half.[1]

What is the lesson here? You must be careful about the sign you ask for because it might bring results you were not expecting.

"Warning Signs" About Signs

When a spiritual truth is overemphasized and taken too far, it can get out of balance and become an error. There is a huge difference between humbly asking God for a sign to confirm His will and putting God to a test by demanding that He meet your expectations. Scripture warns, "You shall not put the Lord your God to the test" (Luke 4:12). It is not wrong to occasionally ask God for a sign, but be careful not to violate scriptural principles or ask Him to do something against His will.

Here are some "warning signs" about signs.

The danger of becoming sign-dependent

Just because you ask God for a sign does not mean He is obligated to give you one. King Herod wanted Jesus to perform a miraculous sign for him, but Jesus would not give in to the king's wishes just to satisfy his curiosity (see Luke 23:8–11).

Some of the religious leaders told Jesus, "Teacher, we want to see a sign from You." Jesus replied, "An evil and adulterous generation craves for a sign; and yet no sign will be given to it but the sign of Jonah the prophet" (Matthew 12:38–39). He had already performed miracles right before their own eyes, which they had refused to believe. Yet they asked Him for even more signs. Since they did not repent after seeing indisputable evidence that He was the Messiah, why should Jesus give them more proof?

Some people think they should ask God for a sign about every decision they need to make. They are sign-dependent, which is dangerous because they will always need to see proof before they will trust God. Although the Lord may occasionally give a sign as confirmation of His will, do not let this be the only factor you consider in making a decision.

The danger of seeing a sign that is not a sign

Some people interpret everything they see as a sign from God. They think He is speaking to them in the oddest of ways. While watching a movie, they will hear an actor quote a line from his script and believe that it is a message from the Lord about a decision they need to make. Although the Lord can speak to you in any way He desires, it is unlikely that He will give you individual guidance through a shooting star, a song on the radio, or a billboard on the highway.

A flight attendant had spent a week's vacation in the Rockies. While there, she met an eligible bachelor who owned a cattle ranch and lived in a log cabin. After a whirlwind one-week romance, Mr. Wonderful proposed to her. Because it all happened so quickly, she decided to return home and think about it.

The next day, during her flight back home, she debated about what to do. To perk up, she stopped in the restroom and splashed some water on her face. Just then the airplane hit some turbulence, which lit up the sign, "Please Return to the Cabin."

And so she did. She took that as a sign from God telling her to return to the mountain cabin and marry him.[2]

I guess that means every time a plane hits turbulence, someone gets married to the owner of a log cabin. She believed in a bathroom sign that was not God's sign, and I seriously doubt they lived happily ever after.

The danger of misinterpreting a sign

Another mistake can be to interpret signs incorrectly. We have all known people who think they have received an unusual message from God, like the farmer who saw "G P" in the clouds. He interpreted it to mean leave the farm and "go preach." After he preached his first sermon, the congregation told him the sign was actually telling him to "go plow."

While the apostle Peter was staying in Joppa, he saw a vision of a sheet coming down from heaven with animals inside it that Jews were forbidden to eat. The vision was repeated three times, and then a voice said, "Get up, Peter, kill and eat." Peter told God, "By no means, Lord, for I have never eaten anything unholy and unclean." The voice answered, "What God has cleansed, no longer consider unholy" (Acts 10:13–15).

Immediately after the message had been given, three Gentile men showed up at the door of the house. If Peter had not correctly interpreted the vision, he would have killed and eaten the three Gentiles.

Instead, the Lord wanted Peter to know that non-Jews, who at that time were considered unacceptable by Jews, would also be included in God's family. Be careful how you interpret signs or you will misunderstand God's intended application for your life.

The Lord may speak to you through a sign, but He may also make His will clear by not giving you a sign. No sign by itself should be taken as absolute proof of God's confirmation, but should be affirmed in other ways, such as biblical truth and wise counsel. As you continue to seek the Lord with an open and willing heart, He will guide you down the correct path.

Now you have learned some key ways that God will guide you through life. Following His leading will result in confidence and peace of mind. In the final section, you will learn how to eliminate any remaining thoughts of worry.

➤ LEARNING TO TRUST

1. A sign is when God does something in a highly unusual way to confirm His will. What does this tell us about His knowledge and power? How can trusting in God's ability keep us from worrying?

2. Why did God give Gideon so many signs? How was his faith tested as a result?

3. What was so unusual about Abraham's servant requesting a woman to water his camels? How do we know with certainty that God brought Rebekah and Isaac together?

4. What are the three "warning signs" about signs?

PART 3

CLAIMING GOD'S PROMISES

When prospectors discovered gold during the California Gold Rush in the 1800s, they had to "stake a claim." Staking a claim meant that they drove posts into the ground to claim the marked property as their own.

God also wants you to stake a claim—on His promises for your life. It is not enough to know what He promises. You must apply the Scriptures to your own situation to make them a reality.

The manager of a large real estate firm interviewed an applicant for a sales job. "Why have you chosen this career?" he asked.

The young man replied, "I dream of making a million dollars in real estate, just like my father."

The manager was impressed. "Your father made a million dollars in real estate?"

"No, but he always dreamed of it."

You might dream of a better life, but until you actually put your faith into action, all your intentions will make absolutely no difference. What good is it to know what to do, but not do it? The problem is not a lack of information, but a lack of application. Information without application is like having the right medicine to cure your sickness but not taking it.

For biblical truth to work in your life, you must put what you have learned into daily practice. In this section, you will learn how to stake your claim on God's promises and apply them to your life.

13

Trusting God to Provide

God created us to have needs. Without them, we
would have no way of knowing our need for God.

—Anonymous

How will I pay my bills? What if I cannot buy groceries? How
will I ever find the right person to marry? If you are human,
you have probably worried about at least one of those things.
Whenever you are faced with a lack of provision, your faith is
being tested. Will you choose to trust God, or will you continue
to torment yourself by worrying?

When Abraham was 75 years old, God promised him that
he would have a son. He only had to wait 25 years before that
baby was born. Several years after the birth of Isaac, the Lord
told Abraham to offer his promised son as a sacrifice.

In obedience to God, Abraham took Isaac to one of the mountains of Moriah and placed him on the altar. As soon as he raised

his knife, a voice from heaven commanded him to stop. At that very moment, a ram was caught by its horns in the thicket. The Lord had provided the ram as a substitute to be offered in the place of his son. Abraham named that place *Jehovah Jireh*, which means, "The LORD will provide" (see Genesis 22:14).

You will come to a place sooner or later when you need the Lord to provide a ram caught in a thicket. While you are waiting for the answer to arrive, you have a choice—either worry or trust.

In the early 1980s, David Smith was the pastor of a small church near Farmington, New Mexico. He faithfully served God but struggled to provide for his wife and small child on his $600 per month salary.

One morning his wife, Jackie, pulled the last can out of the pantry and served him a dish of hominy. Now the cupboard was bare. Literally.

He had often preached on God's faithfulness to provide, but now reality did not match his sermons. This was not in the agreement when he surrendered to full-time ministry.

David got up from the table, bolted through the kitchen door and stomped across the yard next door to his church office. He was furious and wanted the Lord to know exactly how he felt.

"God, You promised to provide for me, but today we are out of food. Where is Your faithfulness that I have been preaching about? Why have You not come through?"

For the next 45 minutes, he kept questioning God about how he was going to feed his family.

And then the phone rang. It was Jackie.

"David, you need to come home right now."

"Why? Is something wrong?"

"You will see when you get here."

David hurried out of the church, but what he saw stopped him in his tracks. A woman was carrying groceries from her car to his front door. Her station wagon was completely filled up to the roof with cans of food and meat. The only space that was not filled was the driver's seat.

"I thought you might need this," the woman explained. "It was on my heart to bring it to you."[1]

Jehovah Jireh—the God who provides. Do you know Him in that way? The Lord will sometimes stretch your faith so you will learn that He will take care of you, even when you are down to the last can in your pantry.

When Jesus sent His disciples to preach in the surrounding cities, He told them, "Take nothing for your trip, neither a walking stick, bag, bread, money, or extra clothes" (Luke 9:3 NCV).

Why would He tell His followers not to take anything? No food? No money? Not even an extra pair of underwear? Why, Lord, why?

Jesus wanted them to experience God's supernatural provision. If they would just do what He asked, He would make sure their every need was met.

The outcome of this experiment is found later in the book of Luke, just before Jesus was betrayed. He asked them to recall the incident where He had sent them out empty-handed: "And He said to them, 'When I sent you out without money belt and bag and sandals, you did not lack anything, did you?' They said, 'No, nothing'" (Luke 22:35).

Jesus knew they did not need to worry because His Father would provide for them, which He did. That same God is your Father as well.

Birds Do Not Get Ulcers

As Jesus was preaching the Sermon on the Mount, He looked at the faces in the crowd and could read their minds. They were worried. Some of them wondered, *What if I starve to death?* Others were thinking, *What if I do not have enough clothes to keep warm when winter comes?*

To calm their fears He said:

"For this reason I say to you, do not be worried about your life, as to what you will eat or what you will drink; nor for your body, as to what you will put on. Is not life more than food, and the body more than clothing? Look at the birds of the air, that they do not sow, nor reap nor gather into barns, and yet your heavenly Father feeds them. Are you not worth much more than they?"

Matthew 6:25–26

In those days no one had refrigerators, freezers, canned food, or well-stocked grocery stores like we have today. They typically did not know where their next meal was coming from. The fear of starvation was at the forefront of their thinking every day.

They did not have packed closets of clothes or a local mall filled with clothing stores. People in those days only owned one or two garments, which were handmade. Clothes were so scarce that God gave this commandment: "If your neighbor gives you his coat as a promise for the money he owes you, you must give it back to him by sunset, because *it is the only cover to keep his body warm.* He has nothing else to sleep in" (Exodus 22:26–27 NCV).

The people living back then were gripped with fear and worry. Jesus pushed them to think outside the box by giving them an object lesson to consider. He pointed to some birds and said, "Do you see those birds sitting on the tree branch? They are not worried about starving to death. You never see birds having nervous breakdowns, do you? They do not say to themselves, *What if I cannot find any worms? What if I cannot find any straw to build my nest? What if a cat eats me?* Birds do not get ulcers or have heart attacks because they never worry."

Then Jesus made a startling statement. It was something they probably had never thought of before. He said, "Your heavenly Father feeds them."

Really? Do you mean that birds do not provide for themselves? God takes responsibility for feeding each one in the entire world? How does He do it?

I have never seen a gigantic hand coming down from heaven, opening the beaks of every bird in the world and dropping in worms. If He does not feed them in that manner, He must do it in another way. He does it by guiding them to their food supply, whether it is worms, seeds, or bugs. And this is why you have never seen a bird starve to death.

Jesus then applied this object lesson to everyone in His audience, hoping they would make the connection. "You are worth more than birds." If the Lord feeds the birds, will He not also take care of His children, who are far more valuable? To drive home the point, He added:

> "Do not worry then, saying, 'What will we eat?' or 'What will we drink?' or 'What will we wear for clothing?' For the Gentiles eagerly seek all these things; for your heavenly Father knows that you need all these things. But seek first His kingdom and His righteousness, and all these things will be added to you. So do not worry about tomorrow; for tomorrow will care for itself. Each day has enough trouble of its own."
>
> Matthew 6:31–34

He tells the Jewish audience, "Whenever you worry, you are acting just like those pagans who do not believe in God. They worry about those things because they do not believe that God will take care of them."

Consider for a moment who is instructing you not to worry. Jesus Christ, the Son of God, and it is impossible for Him to lie. His reputation is at stake. But Jesus is not just telling everyone in the crowd not to worry. He is also speaking to everyone else in the world *who would be reading His words* in generations to come. Jesus knew that His words would be recorded in the Scriptures for all to read, including you.

Do you remember the chapter about God's IQ? To refresh your memory, He knows where every bird is because Jesus said not one falls to ground without the Father knowing about it. He knows the exact number of hairs on your head and every thought in your mind. He knows what you need and how to get the provision to you at the right time.

But there is just one condition. To keep from worrying about provision, you must do something. Jesus told the crowd, "But seek first His kingdom and His righteousness, and all these things will be added to you."

He promised that if you will seek the Lord as your highest priority, you will never have to worry about having your needs met. When you choose to submit yourself to the Lord, He promises to provide for you, just like He guides the birds to their food. Placing your complete trust in God will force your worry to leave.

He again reminds us about what God knows: "For your heavenly Father knows that you need all these things."

Who is *you* in the above Scripture? You! The Lord knows where you are right now, what your situation is and what is best for you. Not only does God know what you need, but "your Father knows what you need *before* you ask Him" (Matthew 6:8).

How Will God Provide During an Economic Crisis?

No one is really worried about starving to death when everything is going well. But if the country were to plunge into an economic depression, nearly everyone would panic. During a national crisis, you cannot put your trust in the economy or the government. Instead, you must choose to place your confidence in Jehovah Jireh, the God who is able to provide for you.

Remember, He knows exactly what you are going through, and if you are submitted to His Lordship, He will make sure your needs are met. It is impossible for God to lie, and here is His promise:

> The LORD knows the days of the blameless, and their inheritance will be forever. They will not be ashamed in the time of evil, and in the days of famine they will have abundance.
>
> Psalm 37:18–19

> Behold, the eye of the LORD is on those who fear Him, on those who hope for His lovingkindness, to deliver their soul from death and to keep them alive in famine.
>
> Psalm 33:18–19

King David wrote this testimony of God's faithfulness for future generations to read:

> I have been young and now I am old, yet I have not seen the righteous abandoned or his children begging for bread.
>
> Psalm 37:25 HCSB

The story of Elijah demonstrates how the Lord can provide food and water during a famine or drought. The prophet Elijah "prayed earnestly that it might not rain, and it did not rain on the earth for three years and six months" (James 5:17).

You might be asking yourself why the prophet would pray for a three-year drought that he would also have to suffer through. He stopped the rain because God wanted evil King Ahab to turn from his sinful ways. Sometimes the Lord will allow a country to suffer hardship so that the people will have a change in heart and surrender their lives to Him. Even when a nation is going through a depression or another crisis, He still promises to make sure His people are provided for.

Learning to follow God's leading will keep you from worrying because He can show you what to do in every situation. After the Lord quit sending rain in Israel, He told Elijah to go to the brook Cherith. "It shall be that you will drink of the brook, and I have commanded the ravens to provide for you there. . . . The ravens brought him bread and meat in the morning and bread and meat in the evening, and he would drink from the brook" (1 Kings 17:4, 6). Because he followed God's guidance, Elijah received the provision he needed.

In the midst of the drought, God *commanded the ravens* to provide for Elijah. This gives us an insight into how the Lord can provide for His people in unusual ways during difficult times. God spoke to the birds and they understood what they needed to do. The same Lord who feeds the birds used the birds to feed the prophet. The ravens went out and found food, and God showed them exactly where to fly to find Elijah.

Do you understand the lesson here? He knows exactly where you are and how to deliver His provision to you.

Every morning and evening the birds flew in breakfast and supper (the first airline food). Elijah did not worry about where they got the food or if they would show up on time. God simply wants you to obey Him, and He will take care of providing for you.

After a while the brook dried up.

> It happened after a while, that the brook dried up, because there was no rain in the land. Then the word of the LORD came to him, saying, "Arise, go to Zarephath, which belongs to Sidon, and stay there; behold, I have commanded a widow there to provide for you."
>
> 1 Kings 17:7–9

Where did that thought come from? As we discussed earlier in this book, God can guide us by speaking to us personally. The Lord did not speak to him about moving somewhere else until after the brook had dried up. He told Elijah the next step to take when he was in need of knowing what to do, and not before then. Elijah's responsibility was to follow God's leading.

God could have commanded the brook to keep flowing, but He allowed this natural resource to run out so Elijah would not stay there. The Lord used the dry creek as a closed door, to divert him in a new direction. When the brook dries up, it is time to move on to a new place.

> God knows exactly where you are and how to deliver His provision to you.

He said, "I have *commanded a widow* there to provide for you." Previously God commanded the ravens to bring him food, but now He commands a widow to provide for him. You would think He would tell a rich person to help Elijah, but instead the Lord chose a poor woman who was down to her last meal.

When you read the story, the widow does not seem to be aware of this command from God (see 1 Kings 17:10–24). All she had left was a handful of flour and a little oil. Nevertheless, she unknowingly did what the Lord commanded and gave it to Elijah.

God can command people to do things for you even though they are unaware of obeying Him. We would never imagine that He would choose ravens and a poor widow to provide for His prophet, but that is what He did. And He can provide for you in ways that you would never expect.

The Lord did not let this woman starve to death after she gave away her last meal. Instead, He supernaturally multiplied what she had given to Elijah. The prophet told her:

"For thus says the LORD God of Israel, 'The bowl of flour shall not be exhausted, nor shall the jar of oil be empty, until the day that the LORD sends rain on the face of the earth.'" So she went and did according to the word of Elijah, and she and he and her household ate for many days. The bowl of flour was not exhausted nor did the jar of oil become empty, according to the word of the LORD which He spoke through Elijah.

1 Kings 17:14–16

The widow let go of what she had, which was the key to receiving God's supernatural provision. This poor woman was willing to give up her last meal to feed the prophet. That sounds like a foolish thing to do, but it was actually the wisest thing she could do. Because she unselfishly gave away her food, the Lord intervened and gave far more back to her.

> God can command people to do things for you even though they are unaware of obeying Him.

Here we learn an important secret about God's kingdom that will never make sense to the natural mind—the Lord will more than replace whatever you give away. Jesus said, "Give, and it will be given to you. They will pour into your lap a good measure—pressed down, shaken together, and running over. For by your standard of measure it will be measured to you in return" (Luke 6:38). He said "they" will pour into your lap, which means He will use a number of different sources to bring provision to you.

God's blessing often comes in response to our cheerfully giving to Him with our tithes and offerings. Solomon writes, "Honor the LORD from your wealth and from the first of all your produce; so your barns will be filled with plenty and your vats will overflow with new wine" (Proverbs 3:9–10).

When you give God the first part of your income and the best of your produce, it proves that you trust Him with your financial situation. The Lord sees your offerings and promises to give back to you with "plenty" and "overflow."

The prophet Malachi verifies the same truth:

> "Bring the whole tithe into the storehouse, so that there may be food in My house, and test Me now in this," says the LORD of hosts, "if I will not open for you the windows of heaven and pour out for you a blessing until it overflows."
>
> Malachi 3:10

Again, God responds to your giving by giving even more back to you. The widow never would have received the miracle of supernatural provision unless she had let go of what she had. In the same way, you will never know the truth of these promises until you start giving offerings to Him by faith.

Sometimes God Provides Beforehand

Sometimes the Lord will provide an abundance during prosperous economic times so that you can save the extra amount for the lean times. Sadly, many people foolishly spend their surplus on lavish lifestyles instead of putting it away for a rainy day. It is wise to save part of your income for emergency situations.

As we saw in a previous chapter, the Pharaoh in Egypt had a couple of dreams about the future. God revealed to Pharaoh that Egypt would have seven years of abundant crops, which would be followed by seven years of famine. Joseph advised Pharaoh to save the extra grain during the seven abundant years to be prepared for the coming seven lean years (see Genesis 41:1–36). Pharaoh wisely heeded his advice.

But what would have happened if Pharaoh had told him, "You want me to save the surplus for seven years? You have got to be kidding me! How do I know for sure that you are telling me the truth? What if you are wrong? What if I save up for seven years and no famine ever comes? No, I won't do it. I want to spend the extra money now so I can build a bigger palace. I want flat-screen TVs with premium channels in every room. Gold hubcaps on all my chariots. Free smartphones for all my slaves!"

> Since God is the only One who knows who and where your future spouse is, you must trust Him to bring you together.

If Pharaoh had spent his profits on extravagant living instead of preparing for the future famine, Egypt and Israel would have perished. Yet many people today are spending their excess income on luxury items instead of saving it. They do not realize that the reason God has blessed them with surplus is so they will keep it for a time when it will be needed in the future.

Is the Lord providing extra income to you right now, but you are not disciplined enough to save it? Are you blowing your money on unnecessary gadgets that you really do not need?

It may be that the Lord is giving you surplus now to set aside for provision for possible lean times. Like Pharaoh, you must be disciplined enough to save it rather than spend it.

How Will You Ever Find the Right Person to Marry?

If you are single, you might want to get married one day. With nearly seven billion people in the world, have you ever thought about how you are going to find the right person to marry? The good news is that you do not need to marry seven billion people. All you need to do is find the right one.

If it is God's will for you to be married, He is the only One who knows who and where your future spouse is, and you must trust Him to bring you together. Instead of worrying about how you will meet the right person, place your complete faith in the Lord and trust that He will take care of it.

If God can lead a fish to a man, then He can lead a woman to a man, or a man to a woman.

Let's review Matthew 17:24–27 one more time. Jesus told Peter to throw a hook into the sea, and the first fish he caught would have a coin in its mouth to pay the temple tax. After Peter threw his fishing line in the Sea of Galilee, the Lord made sure that the right fish bit on his hook. Jesus did not ask Peter to catch all the fish in the sea and sort through them one by one. He told him to go catch the one with a coin in its mouth.

Peter had absolutely no control over which fish would bite on his hook. All he could do was throw out the line, hold the fishing pole and trust what Jesus said. After Peter obeyed what the Lord told him to do, God made the divine connection with the appointed fish. The right fish was in the right place at the right time with the right amount.

Do you see the lesson here? If God can lead a fish to a man, then He can lead a woman to a man, or a man to a woman. Forget about the fact that "there are plenty of fish in the sea." The number of fish available really does not matter because the Lord will take care of matching you with the person He created for you—just like He matched the right fish with Peter.

In the Old Testament, Ruth was gleaning in a field when "she happened to come to the portion of the field belonging to Boaz" (Ruth 2:3). Although she was unaware that the Lord was leading her steps, God led Ruth to that spot in a divine appointment. It was there that she met her future spouse, Boaz.

Ruth was not running all over the world searching for a husband. She was simply doing her everyday duties and the Lord led them together through His providence. She went to the right field at the right time doing the right thing and met the right man. Ruth and Boaz are listed in the genealogy of Jesus (see Matthew 1:5).

We have already seen how God arranged a divine appointment to bring Rebekah to Abraham's servant so that she would marry Isaac (see Genesis 24). If the Lord was able to supernaturally bring people together back then, He is certainly able to do the same thing for you today. If you will completely trust God to do this for you, you will quit worrying about how you will meet your future spouse. Choose to place your faith in the God who loves you and has great plans for your future.

You do not need to go husband hunting or wife seeking, but you do need to "cast out a line" like Peter did. Get involved in Christian fellowship. Find a good church or Bible study group. It may not be the first place that you visit, so keep looking until you find peace in your heart and settle there.

We live in the Internet age, so another way for you to "cast out a line" is by joining a website like eHarmony.com, Christianmingle.com, Christiansingles.com, or a similar site that can match you with members of the opposite sex who share your beliefs and interests. The Internet is a legitimate way that God can introduce people to each other who would never meet otherwise.

The World Wide Web connects millions of people for buying and selling, so why cannot the Lord use that avenue to connect two people for marriage? If your future spouse does not live near you, the Lord could use a website as a connecting point. If that is His plan, God would cause the other person to also join the same website, if that is the avenue He chooses for the divine appointment. A member of my church met her husband through a Christian dating website, and they have been happily married for years.

Do not panic if you are getting older and have not yet met your future spouse. Just think of it as God protecting you from meeting the wrong person. Remember His promise, "No good thing does He withhold from those who walk uprightly" (Psalm 84:11). The Lord's timing is different for everyone. He leads some people to marry at a young age and brings others together later in life.

Just because you have not yet met the right person does not mean that you have missed God's will or that He has forgotten about you. I know a Christian couple who remained single until they met each other, both at age 49. They are happily married and are glad they waited for each other.

You might not be able to do much beyond casting out a line and trusting Him to put the right fish on the hook. Find peace in the fact that God knows all things, has total control over your situation and is able to lead you to the right person without you even planning it. Your responsibility is to love God, go about your daily business and trust Him. He will take care of everything else. "Behold, I am the LORD, the God of all flesh; is anything too difficult for Me?" (Jeremiah 32:27).

Placing your complete trust in God will remove your worry. He promises: "Delight yourself in the LORD; and He will give you the desires of your heart" (Psalm 37:4). That means that He will either fulfill your desire for a spouse, or He will change the desires of your heart to match what He desires for you.

How will you know when you meet the right one? God will put a strong desire inside both you and your future spouse's hearts so that *you will both know* that you are soul mates. I have known some people who knew they found their soul mate the instant their eyes met. But with most people, it takes awhile after meeting before God puts this knowledge within them.

What you do not know is when this divine appointment will happen. It could be tomorrow or it could be years from now. The prophet Isaiah said, "Those who wait for the LORD will gain new strength" (Isaiah 40:31). "Waiting on the Lord" means you will have an *unknown gap of time* between when you ask God to provide and when the provision arrives. It is during this waiting period that you will be the most tempted to either provide for yourself or give up on God. Rest in the Lord and realize the answer is in His hands.

Be assured that God's timing is always perfect, even if you think it should be happening sooner. The Lord could have caused baby Isaac to be born nine months after He gave the promise to Abraham, but His perfect timing was 25 years later.

I know a 44-year-old woman who has been praying for a husband for over twenty years. Even though she has a strong desire to get married, her faith is in God and not in meeting someone. She is committed to following the Lord completely and has decided to enjoy her life, even if she never gets married.

Getting married will not solve all your problems, as is evidenced by the high divorce rate. Being unmarried does have some advantages, so learn to be content in your singleness. Paul, who was single, said, "I have learned to be content in whatever circumstances I am" (Philippians 4:11). Remove the deadline that you have placed on Him and rest in the fact that He has the best planned for you. "Rest in the LORD and wait patiently for Him" (Psalm 37:7). You can pray, "Lord, I have a desire to be married, but You know what is best for me and I want Your will to be done in my life. I will be content with my singleness until the time (if or when) I get married."

The above advice is for those who have a desire to be married. If you do not have that desire and prefer to remain single, you will be perfectly fulfilled with your singleness. Do not get married simply because you are worried about what people think.

The apostle Paul was single and was able to faithfully serve the Lord without having to take care of a family (see 1 Corinthians 7:7–8). Some people who are widowed or divorced prefer to remain single and live happy and fulfilled lives.

Illegal Provision

One of your greatest temptations will be to stop looking to God to meet your needs and to provide for yourself in illegal ways— stealing, cheating on income taxes, excessive borrowing of money when you should not, selling drugs or even selling your body.

When Jesus was tempted in the wilderness, Satan tried to get Him to illegally provide for Himself by turning stones into bread: "And after He had fasted forty days and forty nights, He then became hungry. And the tempter came and said to Him, 'If You are the Son of God, command that these stones become bread'" (Matthew 4:2–3). It was after Jesus became hungry that Satan came to tempt Him. The devil was waiting for Jesus to become vulnerable before he presented his temptation.

Have you ever been hungry at night and then a pizza commercial comes on TV? Within seconds you are on the phone ordering a pizza, which is why advertisers run those commercials at night. You do not see pizza commercials at seven a.m. They know *when* you are going to be hungry, so they run their ads at that time.

Just imagine not eating for forty days. You are doubled over with hunger pains, and then a pizza commercial comes on. The nearest pizza restaurant is miles away, but you have the power to turn a stone into a pizza. Can you see how tempting that would be?

Forty days earlier at His baptism, Jesus heard a voice from heaven say, "This is My beloved Son, in whom I am well-pleased" (Matthew 3:17). His Father identified Jesus as His Son, so the devil tried to get Him to doubt who He was. Satan started each temptation by saying, "If You are the Son of God."

The devil said, "Are You really the Son of God? If You are, then You should have the power to do miracles. It should be easy for You to rearrange the molecules and turn this stone into bread."

Satan probably pointed to a rock that looked exactly like a loaf of bread. When you are hungry, even rocks begin to look good.

Jesus did not say, "Well, I *thought* that I was the Son of God, but now I am not so sure. Maybe I ought to check out My magical powers. Pass Me one of those rocks."

The temptation looked so innocent. No one would get hurt. No one would even know. And He could fulfill His hunger drive—*illegally*. The problem, of course, was that His Father never told Him to start a bakery.

We face the same temptation today: to provide for ourselves instead of waiting for God to provide. Jesus did not provide for Himself illegally, and neither should you. You may have prayed and waited . . . and waited . . . and waited, but the answer still has not come. The devil will come to you at your most vulnerable moment, just like he did Jesus, and will tempt you to take an illegal way to meet your need.

How can you keep from yielding? By placing your total trust in Jehovah Jireh. Do not let your fears force you into making choices you will later regret.

➡ LEARNING TO TRUST

1. When Jesus sent His disciples out to minister in other cities, He told them not to take any money, food or extra clothes with them. (See Luke 9:3.) What did He want them to learn? (See Luke 22:35.)

2. Jesus told us in Matthew 6:25–26 to look at the birds. What can we learn from birds to keep us from worrying?

3. Read Matthew 6:31–34. What did Jesus say we are like when we worry?

4. What unusual thing did God do to make sure Elijah received provision? (See 1 Kings 17:4–6.) What can we learn from this about God providing for our needs?

5. How was it possible for Peter to catch the fish with a coin in its mouth? (See Matthew 17:24–27.) What does this tell us about God's ability to control circumstances?

14

Trusting God for Protection

Safety does not depend on our conception of the absence of danger. Safety is found in God's presence, in the center of His perfect will.

—T. J. Bach

Death is the greatest of all fears, so Jesus gave these comforting words to settle our nerves: "*Do not fear those who kill the body* but are unable to kill the soul; but rather fear Him who is able to destroy both soul and body in hell" (Matthew 10:28).

Did I hear that right? Did Jesus just say not to be afraid when someone wants to kill you? Would that not be a legitimate situation to worry about? According to Jesus, nope. He gave explicit instructions to His followers not to be afraid—even when you are about to be killed!

Jesus was speaking to His disciples and He knew most of them would not die of old age. Nearly all of them would be tortured and killed for their faith, yet Jesus instructed them not to be afraid because their eternal soul was safe. If you are a Christian and obey His instructions, you will not be scared of dying. On the other hand, if you do fear death, you will live in a constant state of worry, and self-preservation will become your highest priority.

Death for the Christian is compared to going to sleep (see John 11:11–13; 1 Corinthians 15:51). It does not hurt to go to sleep, does it? Of course not. And this is why Jesus told His followers not to be afraid of dying. Death is not the worst thing that can happen to you. The worst thing that can happen is to die in your sins and to stand before God without being saved.

However, if you have trusted Jesus to save you from your sins, pure joy awaits you in the next life. Christians who fear death wrongly believe that this life is somehow better than the next life, which is far from the truth. The apostle Paul, who had personally seen heaven, told us it is "very much better" on the other side (see Philippians 1:23; 2 Corinthians 12:2–4). Even so, we live in a troubled world that can make us worried about what might happen in the future.

When Jesus described the signs of the end of the world, He said, "You will be hearing of wars and rumors of wars. *See that you are not frightened*" (Matthew 24:6). Many people are terribly worried about the end of the world, but He specifically told His followers not to be afraid—even during world war. He could not tell us that unless He was in control of those future events and was watching over us.

Once you are determined not to be afraid of your own demise, your worries about being harmed will have no grip on you. Those who have trusted Jesus to save them have been delivered from the fear of death.

Since the children share in flesh and blood, He Himself likewise also partook of the same, that through death He might render powerless him who had the power of death, that is, the devil, and might free those who through fear of death were subject to slavery all their lives.

Hebrews 2:14–15

Claiming God's Promises for Protection

We live on an unredeemed planet where accidents happen and people get hurt. Tragedies will continue to occur until Jesus comes back. Whenever something bad happens, we search for a divine explanation. Why did God allow it? Is He to blame? We want an explanation, thinking that if we just understood, then it would make us feel better.

Jesus encountered many sick people, but He did not stop and explain to every person why they were in that condition. He did not say, "Do you want to know why you got leprosy? Let Me explain. . . . Do you want to understand how that demon got inside you? Here is how. . . ."

Since Jesus did not give reasons as to why people got hurt, we should not try to come up with our own explanation. It is wrong to try to make an evaluation when you do not have all the facts. You must not presuppose that every accident or tragedy is because God caused it to happen or that He was punishing people for their sins. Jesus said that is not the case.

In Jesus' day, some people had been murdered by Pilate, while others were killed in an accident. Yet Jesus explained that neither happened because they brought it upon themselves.

> Now on the same occasion there were some present who reported to Him about the Galileans whose blood Pilate had mixed with their sacrifices. And Jesus said to them, "Do you suppose that these Galileans were greater sinners than all other Galileans because they suffered this fate? *I tell you, no.* . . . Or do you

suppose that those eighteen on whom the tower in Siloam fell and killed them were worse culprits than all the men who live in Jerusalem? *I tell you, no*, but unless you repent, you will all likewise perish."

Luke 13:1–5

The Galileans who were offering sacrifices were butchered by an evil man. The eighteen people were killed in an accident when the tower fell on them, apparently during its construction. Some people were saying that they all died because God caused it to happen. Jesus explained that those tragedies were not an act of divine retribution due to their sinfulness.

> Although you cannot see God, you can see His promises recorded in the Bible.

We live in a world where it is possible to be harmed in many different ways. Protection is not guaranteed. However, the Scriptures tell us that many injuries can be prevented by asking for God's protection.

Ezra was about to lead a group of people through a dangerous area and he knew they would very likely be attacked. He fasted and prayed, asking for God's protection.

Then I proclaimed a fast there at the river of Ahava, that we might humble ourselves before our God *to seek from Him a safe journey for us, our little ones*, and all our possessions. For I was ashamed to request from the king troops and horsemen to protect us from the enemy on the way, because we had said to the king, "The hand of our God is favorably disposed to all those who seek Him, but His power and His anger are against all those who forsake Him."

Ezra 8:21–22

Ezra had told the king that God would take care of them, so he refused to ask for a convoy of the king's troops and horsemen. There is nothing wrong with asking for human protection, but Ezra knew that traveling through the enemy territories was so dangerous only God could properly guard them. Instead of worrying, he placed his complete trust in the Lord for safety. Here is what Ezra recorded after he had arrived:

> Then we journeyed from the river Ahava on the twelfth of the first month to go to Jerusalem; and the hand of our God was over us, and *He delivered us from the hand of the enemy and the ambushes by the way.*
>
> Ezra 8:31

Ezra's journey to Jerusalem took about four months, and the Lord supernaturally prevented every attack and ambush from the enemies so that the caravan arrived safely. His trust in God through prayer and fasting undoubtedly brought a shield of divine protection.

We are trusting in an invisible God to watch over us and so we must take His protection by faith. One little boy said, "Air bags are kind of like God. You know they're there to protect you, but you can't see them."

Although you cannot see God, you can see His promises recorded in the Bible. He wants you to claim them, which means to make them your own by believing in them. The fulfillment of the promise is up to God, not you. The book of Joshua says, "Not one of the good promises which the LORD had made to the house of Israel failed; all came to pass" (Joshua 21:45).

God does not want His children to be worried about what might happen, so He promises to give us His supernatural peace. Jesus said, "Peace I leave with you, My peace I give to you; not as the world gives do I give to you. *Let not your heart be troubled, neither let it be afraid*" (John 14:27 NKJV). Worry comes when you "let" your heart be troubled and afraid.

Here are a few of God's promises concerning protection that He wants you to believe in your heart.

> But he who listens to me shall live securely and will be at ease from the dread of evil.
>
> Proverbs 1:33

> The name of the LORD is a strong tower; the righteous runs into it and is safe.
>
> Proverbs 18:10

> The LORD is my light and my salvation; whom shall I fear? The LORD is the defense of my life; whom shall I dread? . . . Though a host encamp against me, my heart will not fear; though war arise against me, in spite of this I shall be confident.
>
> Psalm 27:1, 3

> I will lift up my eyes to the mountains; from where shall my help come? My help comes from the LORD, who made heaven and earth. . . . The LORD will protect you from all evil; He will keep your soul. The LORD will guard your going out and your coming in from this time forth and forever.
>
> Psalm 121:1–2, 7–8

> Who is there to harm you if you prove zealous for what is good?
>
> 1 Peter 3:13

Psalm 91 is the most detailed chapter concerning God's protection:

> I will say to the LORD, "My refuge and my fortress, My God, in whom I trust!" For it is He who delivers you from the snare of the trapper and from the deadly pestilence. . . . You will

not be afraid of the terror by night, or of the arrow that flies by day; of the pestilence that stalks in darkness, or of the destruction that lays waste at noon. A thousand may fall at your side and ten thousand at your right hand, but it shall not approach you. . . . For you have made the LORD, my refuge, even the Most High, your dwelling place. No evil will befall you, nor will any plague come near your tent. For He will give His angels charge concerning you, to guard you in all your ways. They will bear you up in their hands, that you do not strike your foot against a stone. . . . "Because he has loved Me, therefore I will deliver him; I will set him securely on high, because he has known My name. He will call upon Me, and I will answer him; I will be with him in trouble; I will rescue him and honor him. With a long life I will satisfy him and let him see My salvation."

vv. 2–3, 5–7, 9–12, 14–16

When you are tempted to worry, speak God's promises out loud. Declare with your mouth what He has promised to you. "Let us hold fast the confession of our hope without wavering, for He who promised is faithful" (Hebrews 10:23).

When Protection Is Not Promised

God's protection is not guaranteed if you foolishly walk down a dark alley in a rough neighborhood, or jump in front of a moving car. Making foolish decisions while assuming that God will protect you is called presumption. Presumption tempts God, trying to force Him to act against His will.

When the devil tempted Jesus, he tried to get Him to force the Father to come to His aid. In the last chapter, we saw that Satan tempted Jesus in regard to *provision*. When that did not work, he tempted Him in the area of *protection*. The devil took Him to the pinnacle of the temple and tried to get Him to jump off.

Why would Jesus be tempted to do something as crazy as jumping off the temple? Many of the Jews expected the Messiah to appear suddenly by floating down into the temple area. They based this belief on Malachi 3:1, which says, "'And the Lord, whom you seek, will suddenly come to His temple; and the messenger of the covenant, in whom you delight, behold, He is coming,' says the LORD of hosts." If Jesus jumped off the top of the temple and the angels safely carried Him to the bottom unhurt, He would receive instant acceptance as the Messiah.

> Satan wanted Jesus to trust in the **ability** of God, but to ignore the **will** of God.

It made perfect sense. Quick. Easy. Impressive.

The devil even quoted the perfect Scripture verse from Psalm 91 to get Him to jump:

> "If You are the Son of God, throw Yourself down; for it is written, 'He will command His angels concerning You'; and 'On their hands they will bear you up, so that You will not strike Your foot against a stone.'"
>
> Matthew 4:6

Satan said, "If You really believe God's Word, You will trust Him to protect You if You jump off. God promises to send His angels to catch You and bear You up with their hands."

This was one of the trickiest temptations of them all because the devil tempted Jesus *with Scripture*. What an unlikely tool to tempt someone with—the very words of God! No one would suspect that the Word of God, taken out of context, could be an instrument of temptation.

This is one of those rare cases where the devil wanted Jesus to trust His Father. Satan wanted Him to trust in the *ability* of God, but to ignore the *will* of God.

Jesus answered, "On the other hand, it is written, 'You shall not put the LORD your GOD to the test'" (Matthew 4:7). To say it another way, you cannot force God's hand to work against God's heart. The hand of God and the heart of God work together, not apart.

If Jesus had jumped off the temple, He would have obeyed Satan, not His Father. Angels are not obligated to catch people who follow Satan's instructions. And if the angels would not have caught the Son of God, it is unlikely they will protect those who act irresponsibly.

I have seen a lot of people jumping off temples, obeying the devil's suggestions. Then someone else has to clean up the mess at the bottom. God does not promise protection for those who ignore His will and live recklessly. His promises can be claimed by those who obey Him.

The Protection of God's Presence

Scripture draws a correlation between God's presence and fear's absence. Fear must leave when God is present with someone.

- David said, "Even though I walk through the valley of the shadow of death, I fear no evil, *for You are with me*" (Psalm 23:4).

- God told Joshua, "Do not tremble or be dismayed, for the LORD *your God is with you* wherever you go" (Joshua 1:9).

- Moses told Israel, "The LORD is the one who goes ahead of you; *He will be with you*. He will not fail you or forsake you. Do not fear or be dismayed" (Deuteronomy 31:8).

- Again the Lord says, "Do not fear, *for I am with you*; do not anxiously look about you, for I am your God. I will strengthen you, surely I will help you" (Isaiah 41:10).

When you walk with God, He is with you. Having God's presence with you also means having His protection. That is why when you choose to trust the Lord you do not need to worry. It will help you to confess out loud, "Lord, I believe that You are with me, so I am not going to worry or be afraid." This is not merely positive thinking, but acknowledging the reality of God's promises.

Once you place your trust in the Lord, you will sleep peacefully at night without worrying about what will happen to you. Proverbs 3:23–24 says, "You will walk in your way securely and your foot will not stumble. When you lie down, you will not be afraid; when you lie down, your sleep will be sweet." David adds, "In peace I will both lie down and sleep, for You alone, O LORD, make me to dwell in safety" (Psalm 4:8).

Jesus said, "Do not keep worrying" (Luke 12:29). Do you get the idea that God *never* wants you to fret? That is what He said. Think how much you would enjoy life if you could eliminate all worrying.

Yes, it can happen. But only if you will rest on God's promises.

➡ LEARNING TO TRUST

1. What does it mean to "claim" God's promises for yourself?

2. Why did Jesus tell His followers not to be afraid of being killed? (See Matthew 10:28.) How can conquering the fear of death set you free from worry?

3. How do you think God protected Ezra's caravan as they traveled through a very dangerous area for four months? (See Ezra 8:21–22, 31.)

4. Read Psalm 91. Why do you need to believe that God is in control before you can rest on this promise of protection?

5. How does the awareness of God's presence with you keep you from being afraid? (See Psalm 23:4; Joshua 1:9.)

15

Releasing Your Worry

> I have spent most of my life worrying about things
> that never happened.
>
> —Mark Twain

Let's go over the checklist.

Trusting that God is in control even when you do not understand. Check.

Following God's instructions to the best of your knowledge. Check.

Believing that God will provide and protect you no matter how your circumstances appear. Check.

Now you must learn to control what you think about. The sure cure for worry is found in a disciplined thought life. The Lord has granted you an amazing privilege—the ability to control your thoughts.

Worry and trust are both assumptions that you make about the future. Worry assumes the worst will occur. Trust assumes

God has the best planned for you. You get to choose which one you will believe and what thoughts will run your life. What you decide will determine whether you will live happily ever after, or if you will be miserable until your dying day.

Time Zones in Your Mind

Although you can only live in the present, your mind can transport you in a mental time machine to another time zone. Does your mind ever get stuck in the past time zone? Perhaps you have been reminiscing about good memories, longing to live back there. On the other hand, you could be thinking about a hurt from the past, something bad that you did or an issue that has not been resolved. You keep visiting the painful past, even though it makes more sense not to go there.

Maybe your mind travels in the other direction to the future time zone and lingers there. That is not necessarily bad. Not all thoughts of the future are about worry. Hope, vision and making plans are good reasons to think about the future.

The prophet Jeremiah told Israel, "'For I know the plans that I have for you,' declares the LORD, 'plans for welfare and not for calamity to give you a future and a hope'" (Jeremiah 29:11). God also has good plans for your life to give you hope. However, worry sends your mind into the future so you will agonize about the horrible things that *might* happen.

> Your feelings respond to whatever you have been thinking about.

When your mind is parked in the future time zone, you are actually adding a heavy burden to your soul that you do not need to be carrying. It is good to make plans for the future, but do not get stuck there. Bring your thoughts back to the present.

Concentrate on what the Lord wants you to do today instead of fretting about every worst-case scenario for the next 25 years.

Your Thoughts Affect Your Feelings

What you think about has a powerful effect on the way you feel. Your feelings respond to whatever you have been thinking about. If you are happy, it is because you have been thinking happy thoughts. If you are sad, you have been thinking sad thoughts. If you are depressed, you have been dwelling on depressing thoughts. If you are worried, it is because you have been meditating on fearful thoughts of the future. Stop mulling over what might happen to you, and your worrying will cease.

If you go to a movie theater and watch a comedy, it puts you in a jovial mood. Although you know the movie is not reality, it still affects you emotionally. A suspenseful movie will cause you to be tense. A sad movie brings tears to your eyes. What you see on the movie screen is affecting your emotions.

Your mind works like a screen in a theater, and your imaginations are the movies being projected on it. Worry makes every imagined tragedy appear as though it is actually happening. What you are viewing is fiction, but you are convinced the horror movie in your mind is real. And you are the star of the movie! What you are watching is happening to you.

You do not have to keep torturing yourself by watching it. Stop the film. The apostle Paul gave instructions about how to turn off the projector: "Casting down imaginations, and every high thing that is exalted against the knowledge of God, and bringing every thought into captivity to the obedience of Christ" (2 Corinthians 10:5 ASV). You can end the horror movie by casting down the imagination.

Tell those tormenting thoughts to leave in Jesus' name. If you do not forcefully take a stand, the movies in your mind will continue torturing you. It will be a never-ending horror film. Taking authority over the frightening imaginations is the only way to make those worrisome thoughts leave. After casting down the imaginary worries, you must bring "every thought into captivity to the obedience of Christ" to start thinking differently.

If you pull weeds out of the ground, they quickly come back if grass is not immediately planted to take up the empty space. Once you pull the worry weeds out of your mind, start planting grass by meditating on positive, uplifting thoughts every day.

Again, Doctor Paul gives the prescription for the sure cure: "Finally, brethren, whatever is true, whatever is honorable, whatever is right, whatever is pure, whatever is lovely, whatever is of good repute, if there is any excellence and if anything worthy of praise, *dwell on these things*" (Philippians 4:8).

Keep your mind occupied with positive thoughts and it will be difficult for the negative thoughts to gain access. When a sponge is fully absorbed with water, it cannot hold any more. Casting down fearful imaginations is like squeezing filthy water out of the sponge, and meditating on uplifting thoughts is like fully absorbing the sponge with clean water. Thinking fearful thoughts will make you afraid, but thinking joyful thoughts will make you joyful.

Being genuinely thankful to God is a powerful weapon that disarms worry. Instead of worrying about starving to death, start thanking God for all the food He has already given you for your entire life. "In everything give thanks, for this is God's will for you in Christ Jesus" (1 Thessalonians 5:18). The Lord loves to be thanked, and He will keep sending blessings to those who truly appreciate what they have been given.

Casting Your Worries to the Lord

Approximately 92 percent of the things you worry about will never happen. That is the good news. But you are probably wondering about the other 8 percent. What about that? Those future situations will either not be as bad as you think, or God will give you the grace to get through them. That takes care of all of your problems.

King David was bombarded with a host of things he could worry about. Saul was constantly trying to kill him. He fought in bloody battles against the Philistines. His own son Absalom conspired to turn the people of Israel against him and take over his throne. After the Amalekites burned down the city of Ziklag and kidnapped his family, his own men talked about stoning him (see 1 Samuel 30:1–6). He was in constant danger of being murdered or killed in battle.

Despite all the perils he faced, he wrote, "I sought the LORD, and He answered me, and *delivered me from all my fears*" (Psalm 34:4).

David sought the Lord as the highest priority in his life. In response, God set him free from all his fears. Every single one of them. Would you like to experience that same peace in your life? You can, if you will practice the principle of transference.

1. Transfer your trust to God

Everyone trusts in something, whether it is money, a job, the government, or another person. "Some trust in chariots and some in horses, but we trust in the name of the LORD our God" (Psalm 20:7 NIV). We can even subconsciously place our trust in our own abilities. As long as we can handle everything, we have no need to trust God. But when things are spinning out of our control, we start worrying because we cannot handle the situation.

Proverbs 3:5 says, "Trust in the LORD with all your heart and do not lean on your own understanding." When you put your complete trust in God, you will stop trying to figure everything out. No more wondering about what is going to happen or how things will turn out. Let the Lord worry about that.

Trust is having confidence in a person. In order to trust God, you must transfer your trust from yourself to Him. David said, "When I am afraid, I will put my trust in You. . . . In God I have put my trust; I shall not be afraid" (Psalm 56:3–4). He transferred his trust to the Lord instead of trusting in himself and living in torment.

You can release your problem by letting go and casting it into God's hands.

David *put* his trust in God. To "put" means to relocate from one place to another. You take money from your bank account and *put* it in your purse. You take fuel out of the gas pump and *put* it in your car. So when you *put* your trust in the Lord, you transfer your confidence from yourself to Him.

I took swimming lessons at the local neighborhood pool when I was a kid. I remember grabbing the side of the pool and kicking my legs as the instructor held me up. Piece of cake. *This is easy,* I thought.

But then came the hard part—learning how to float!

I would eventually be going into water over my head, and the instructor would not be there to hold me up. The fear of drowning suddenly gripped my heart.

My instructor told me that the water would hold me up, but I was not so sure that I believed him. In my mind, floating in water seemed to defy the law of gravity. Whenever I stood in the pool in a vertical position, I knew the water did not hold me up. Now I was supposed to believe that if I was lying in a horizontal position on top of the water I would not sink?

The teacher took me to the middle of the pool, where the water was up to my neck. He held me up in a horizontal position and then let go. Immediately I felt myself going under, so I started wildly splashing water as I quickly stood up. It did *not* hold me up like he had said!

Over the next few weeks, I tried floating. And I tried hard. Every time I would try to lie horizontally on the surface, my legs would drop down to stand up. Not once did the water hold me up. I thought I would never learn.

Then one day, I gave up *trying* to float and just went limp. Much to my surprise, I floated for the first time in my life— and it did not require any effort on my part. I quit trusting in my own ability to float and surrendered to the water to hold me up.

Learning to trust God is like learning how to float in water. We try really hard to trust Him, but it does not work. So we keep trying to work up our faith, hoping that one day we will be able to trust. Finally, we quit struggling and inwardly go limp. We stop being self-dependent and put our complete dependence on Him by saying, "Lord, I can't do this, so I'm counting on You to hold me up." When you do this, you have just transferred your trust to God.

2. Transfer your problems to God

Now that you have transferred your trust to God, you can transfer your problems to Him. "Don't worry about anything; instead, pray about everything; tell God your needs, and don't forget to thank him for his answers" (Philippians 4:6 TLB). Instead of worrying, release your problem into God's hands through prayer.

Give the Lord your concerns. "Casting all your care on Him, because He cares about you" (1 Peter 5:7 HCSB). When you throw a ball to someone, you have to let go of it. You can release your problem by letting go and casting it into God's hands. Now it is no longer in your hands, but in His.

If you are worried about a national crisis such as a terrorist attack or an economic depression, you can pray, "Lord, I have given my life to You, and You told me that I do not need to fear death because it's like going to sleep, and life in heaven is far better than here on earth. You have promised to provide for me as long as I am alive, even during times of scarcity. Since it is impossible for You to lie, I will not worry about the future but will enjoy what You have called me to do today."

Perhaps you are worried about flying in an airplane. Even though the odds of being killed in an airline crash are one in 29.4 million, you think that you have picked the doomed flight.[1] If you had to bet $10,000 on whether or not the plane would crash, which one would you bet on? Obviously, you would bet on it not happening due to the odds. But whenever you worry, you are placing your bet on the disaster occurring, even though the odds are overwhelmingly against it.

Remember the sure cure for worry—trusting God forces out worry. Transfer your worry to Him by saying, "Lord, I believe that You will prevent me from boarding this plane if something bad is going to happen. I will make plans to get on this flight and I know that if I get on that plane, it is a sign of assurance from You that You will get me safely to my destination."

Are you worried about an illness or another health problem? You can pray, "Lord, I thank You for doctors, hospitals and medicine. I know they can help me with some of my health problems but not all of them. I recognize You as my Great Physician and the One who brings healing. Show me my part in taking care of the health of my body and I ask You to heal me, even when it is beyond the doctor's ability" (see Mark 5:24–34; Psalm 103:3).

Suppose your situation is so dire that you need a miraculous answer. You can pray, "Lord, I surrender myself completely to You and place my situation in Your hands. I know all things are possible with You, so I humbly ask for a miracle. I will give You all the credit and will boldly tell everyone that You are the

One who answered my prayer when I had no hope." (See Luke 18:27, where Jesus said, "The things that are impossible with people are possible with God.")

Maybe you are worried about your children. What can you do to find peace of mind? Put them in the Lord's hands and pray for them.

When Pharaoh ordered all the male Hebrew babies to be killed, Jochebed put baby Moses in a tar-covered wicker basket and placed it in the reeds by the Nile River (see Exodus 2:3–9). Moses could have easily been eaten by a crocodile or swept downstream, but Jochebed placed him in God's hands and trusted Him with her baby's future.

The Lord responded to her faith by arranging a divine appointment. He led the daughter of Pharaoh down to the river at just the right time, and she found the baby. Moses' sister Miriam went to her and asked, "Shall I go and call a nurse for you from the Hebrew women that she may nurse the child for you?" (v. 7). Miriam ran to get Jochebed, the mother of Moses. Pharaoh's daughter paid her wages to nurse her own baby, and Moses was protected from Pharaoh's edict.

Have you placed your children in God's hands? Just as Jochebed let go of Moses and put him in the Lord's hands, you must do the same with your children. Perhaps you have a wayward child that you are worried about. Maybe your child is in a dangerous situation and needs God's protection. In your heart, turn your child over to the Lord and let Him take care of the situation. If he or she is rebellious, the change in your child's behavior might not happen instantly, but will happen eventually if you will trust Him.

You can pray, "Lord, I let go and place my child in Your hands. I trust You for protection. I'm going to stop worrying because I trust You to take control over what I cannot do. Thank You for having good plans for my child."

How do you know if you are trusting God? If you are relaxed and have peace of mind instead of being tense and stressed out, then you have arrived at the place of trust.

Enjoy the Journey

Have you chosen to enjoy your life? Worry will always drain your joy and happiness. That in itself is a good enough reason to decide to stop worrying. You are not enjoying life!

The Lord did not put you on this planet to watch you be tormented with worry. He wants you to enjoy your journey through this life. Jesus said, "These things I have spoken to you so that My joy may be in you, and that your joy may be made full" (John 15:11). He promised to put *His* joy inside you, which means that a significant part of His will for you is to enjoy life. You cannot have joy and worry at the same time.

Stop torturing yourself. Surrender your life to the Lord. Place your complete trust in Him. Live one day at a time. Control what you think about. Release your problems to God through prayer. And enjoy the rest of your life to its fullest.

Now you know the sure cure for worry. All that is left is for you to apply it.

➡ LEARNING TO TRUST

1. Your thoughts will affect the way you feel. What kind of thoughts should be occupying your mind? (See Philippians 4:8.)

2. What are you supposed to do when frightening imaginations torment you? (See 2 Corinthians 10:5.)

3. Approximately 92 percent of the things you worry about
   will never happen. How does God take care of the other
   8 percent?

4. David said, "When I am afraid, I will put my trust in
   You. . . . In God I have put my trust; I shall not be afraid"
   (Psalm 56:3–4). How do you transfer your trust to God?

5. How do you transfer your problems to God? (See Philippians 4:6–7; 1 Peter 5:7.)

Notes

Chapter 1: Trusting in an Invisible God

1. Pete and Robin Shultis have been my friends for more than 25 years. Special thanks to them for sharing their story.

Chapter 2: Divine Appointments

1. I served on staff at the Family Church with Max Wilkins.
2. "William Paton Mackay's Testimony" http://maranatha777.wordpress.com/2008/06/28/william-paton-mackays-testimony/.
3. "The Story of Dr. W. P. Mackay and the Faithfulness of God," www.cobblestoneroadministry.org/2007/SermonStory_William_P_Mackay_FaithfulnessOfGod.html; Robert J. Morgan, *More Real Stories for the Soul* (Nashville: Thomas Nelson Publishers, 2000), 137–140; and *Stem Publishing*, "William Paton Mackay, 1839–1885," www.stempublishing.com/hymns/biographies/mackay.html.
4. *Faith & Renewal*, March/April 1993, 29.
5. Bob Mumford, *Take Another Look at Guidance* (Plainfield, N.J.: Logos International, 1971), 24.

Chapter 3: Indisputable Proof God Controls the World

1. For a detailed explanation of this prophecy that shows the prophetic clock, I recommend *Daniel's Prophecy of the 70 Weeks* by Alva McClain.
2. Peter Stoner, *Science Speaks* (Chicago: Moody Press, 1963).

Chapter 4: God's IQ

1. BookRags, "Marilyn vos Savant Biography," www.bookrags.com/biography/marilyn-vos-savant/.

2. John P., One Man's Blog, "The Massive List of Genius–People With the Highest IQ," November 8, 2007, http://onemansblog.com/2007/11/08/the-massive -list-of-genius-people-with-the-highest-iq/. Note that for those who lived before IQ tests were available or never took one, these are estimates.

3. European Space Agency, "How many stars are there in the Universe?" February 23, 2004, www.esa.int/esaSC/SEM75BS1VED_extreme_0.html.

4. Dan Vergano, "Universe holds billions more stars than previously thought," *USA Today,* December 1, 2010, http://usatoday30.usatoday.com/tech/science/ space/2010-12-01-dwarf-stars_N.htm.

5. "Star survey reaches 70 sextillion," July 23, 2003, www.cnn.com/2003/TECH/ space/07/22/stars.survey/.

6. Gyles Brandreth, *Your Vital Statistics* (Lyle Stuart, 1986), 22.

Chapter 5: Placing Your Life in God's Hands

1. C. W. Bess, *Nothing Can Separate Us* (Nashville: Broadman Press, 1986), 132.

Chapter 6: Where Did That Thought Come From?

1. Charlie Greer, "What Are You Thinking?," www.hvacprofitboosters.com/ Tips/Tip_Archive/tip_archive7.html.

2. Peter Lord, *Hearing God* (Grand Rapids: Chosen Books, 2011), 73.

Chapter 7: Guidance Through Dreams

1. Charles Shepson, *How to Know God's Will* (Camphill, Pa.: Christian Publications, Inc., 1998), 28–30.

2. Jeremy Taylor, "Creative Impulse in Dreams," www.jeremytaylor.com/pages/ creativity.html.

3. Richard Innes, *Daily Encounter,* July 27, 2012, quoting Jim Green, Executive Director of The *Jesus* Film Project, a division of Campus Crusade for Christ International. Monthly report letter, July 8, 2005, www.actsweb.org/daily.php?id=1022.

Chapter 8: God Speaks Through Others

1. Charles Swindoll, *Insight for Living,* April 8, 1991.

2. Donald Grey Barnhouse, *Acts: An Expositional Commentary* (Grand Rapids: Zondervan, 1979), 189–191.

Chapter 9: Following Your Heart

1. Prayer Tower, *George Mueller: Man of Prayer,* "How to Know God's Will," www.prayertower.org/GeoMueller.htm.

2. *Our Daily Bread,* July 12, 1995.

Chapter 10: Man's Rejection Can Be God's Direction

1. Rick Warren, "Three responses to trouble," *Ministry ToolBox,* Issue #322, August 1, 2007.

Chapter 11: Open and Closed Doors

1. Numbers 22; Deuteronomy 23:4–5; Joshua 13:22; 24:9; Nehemiah 13:2; Micah 6:5; 2 Peter 2:15; Jude 1:11; Revelation 2:14.

Chapter 12: Pay Attention to the Signs

1. John Walvoord and Roy Zook, editors, *The Biblical Knowledge Commentary* (Wheaton, Ill.: Victor Books, 1986), 580. See Heb. 11:37.

2. *Reader's Digest,* January 1981, 118.

Chapter 13: Trusting God to Provide

1. David Smith was my roommate when I attended Southwestern Baptist Theological Seminary.

Chapter 15: Releasing Your Worry

1. This statistic applies when flying on one of the "top 30 airlines with the best accident rates," www.planecrashinfo.com/cause.htm.

Kent Crockett graduated from Texas A&M University and Southwestern Baptist Theological Seminary. After graduating from seminary, he and his wife, Cindy, planted a church in Garden City, Kansas, where he was pastor for eighteen years. In 1997 he wrote his first book, *The 911 Handbook*, which became a CBA bestseller.

Kent has also worked as an editor for a Christian publishing company, as director of development at Brewton-Parker College in Georgia and as a pastor in churches in Florida and Alabama. He is currently the discipleship pastor at Journey Church in Prattville, Alabama. His other books include *Making Today Count for Eternity, 10 Secrets to Life's Biggest Challenges, I Once Was Blind but Now I Squint* and *Slaying Your Giants*.

Kent enjoys spending time with his family, going to the beach and following Texas A&M sports. His life's goal is to be pleasing to the Lord in all things, to make today count for eternity and to finish well in running the race of life. You can contact him through his website, www.kentcrockett.com, or email kent@kentcrockett.com.

How Prepared Are You?

ALSO FROM KENT CROCKETT

Certain kinds of things just happen—and they happen to everyone. Trouble at work, conflicts in relationships, money problems, criticism, temptation—these are just a few of the situations we all find ourselves in. The big question, then, is this: Are you prepared for them? When the storms hit, are you and your loved ones ready to survive—and even thrive?

In addition to identifying ten inevitable challenges you will face, bestselling author and respected pastor Peter Lord also reveals *the secrets to overcoming them.* Learn how to prepare and live victoriously no matter what your circumstances are.

10 Secrets to Life's Biggest Challenges
by Peter Lord with Kent Crockett